French Silver

1450–1825

French Silver

1450-1825

BY
FRANK DAVIS

ARTHUR BARKER LIMITED
5 WINSLEY STREET LONDON W1

To the memory of N. G. D.

SBN 213 17803 6

PRINTED IN GREAT BRITAIN
BY WILLMER BROTHERS LIMITED
BIRKENHEAD

Contents

List of Illustrations

18 Silver-gilt Bottle, 12 ins. high, attributed Noël Delacroix, c. 1581–2. *Musée du Louvre.*

19 Ewer and dish by Louis Regnard, 1747. *S. J. Phillips.*

20 Gold Casket, no marks, c. 1645. *Musée du Louvre.*

21 Gold Beaker, first half seventeenth century. *M. Stavros Niarchos.*

22 Inkstand, length 6⅝ ins., weight 22 oz. 14 dwts. Avignon, c. 1670. *Private Collection.*

23, 24 Beaker, mark illegible. Paris, 1731–2. *Hermitage, Leningrad.*

25 Beaker by François Balzac. Paris, 1737. *Firestone Collection.*

26, 27 Silver-gilt Beaker by Jean Stahl. Strasbourg, 1754. *Victoria and Albert Museum.* Crown Copyright.

28, 29 Silver-gilt Cadenas by Henry Auguste. Paris, 1804. *Private Collection.*

30 Marie-Antoinette's *Nécessaire de Voyage*, case of mahogany, contents of silver, porcelain and ivory. *Musée du Louvre..*

31, 32 Basin by Claude II Ballin, 1712–13. *Residenzmuseum, Munich.*

33, 34 Casket by Claude II Ballin, 1712–13. *Residenzmuseum, Munich.*

35, 36 & 37 Gold-mounted Rock-crystal Ewer and Basin, height 18·4 cm., maker unknown, 1727–32. *The Wallace Collection.*

38 The Chatsworth Toilet Service by Pierre Prévost, 1670–1. *Chatsworth Trustees.*

39, 40 A Box from the Chatsworth Toilet Service.

41, 42 Pair of Silver-gilt Flasks, maker's mark PDN with a fleur-de-lis, height 6⅞ ins. Paris, 1669–70. *Victoria and Albert Museum.*

43 Silver-gilt Basin, 34 cm., attributed to Nicolas Besnier, 1717–22. *Musée du Louvre.*

44 Toilet Service by Sébastien Igonet, Alexis Loir III, Antoine Lebrun and Étienne Pollet. Paris, 1738–39. *Detroit Institute of Arts.*

45, 46 Toilet Service by François-Thomas Germain, 1765–66. *Hermitage, Leningrad.*

47 Glove Tray, height 1⅝ ins., eighteenth century. *Metropolitan Museum, New York.*

48 Ewer and Basin by Léopold Antoine. Paris, 1727–29. *Metropolitan Museum, New York.*

49, 50 Silver-gilt Ewer and Basin. Paris, 1809–19. *M. Stavros Niarchos.*

51 Ewer and Basin by Jean Fauche. Paris, 1739–42. *Metropolitan Museum, New York.*

52 Box, height 3¾ ins., by Nicolas Besnier, 1714. *Firestone Collection.*

53 Soap Box, height 3 ins., by Pierre Prévost, 1729. *Firestone Collection.*

54 Soap Box by Pierre Hannier, 1730. *Christie's.*

55 Ewer and Basin, height 9½ ins., by Sébastien Igonet, 1733. *Christie's.*

56, 57 Terrine, one of a pair from the Berkeley Castle Service by Jacques Roëttiers, 1737. *M. Stavros Niarchos.*

91 Shell-shaped Dish by Louis Regnard, 1753–54. *Metropolitan Museum, New York, Wentworth Bequest.*

92 Pair of Shell-shaped Dishes by Jacques-Nicolas Roëttiers, 1772–73. *Metropolitan Museum, New York, Wentworth Bequest.*

93 Mustard Barrel, height 3½ ins., by Aymé Joubert, 1727. *Firestone Collection.*

94 Mustard Pot, 3⅝ ins., one of a pair by Louis Regnard, 1740–41. *Metropolitan Museum, New York, Wentworth Bequest.*

95 Mustard Pot, 5⁷⁄₁₆ ins., by Henry Adnet, 1717–22. *Metropolitan Museum, New York, Wentworth Bequest.*

96 Mustard Pot by Guillaume Egée, 1748–49. *Metropolitan Museum, New York, Wentworth Bequest.*

97 Two-handled Bowl, diameter 11 cm. Morlaix, c. 1700. *M. Stavros Niarchos.*

98A & B Wine Taster by R.-L. Charpentier. Rambervilliers, c. 1750. *M. Stavros Niarchos.*

99, 100 Sugar Bowl, height 5⅝ ins., by Simon le Bastier, 1711–12. *Victoria and Albert Museum. Crown Copyright.*

101 Spice Box with Grater, height 2¼ ins., by Charles-François Croze, 1719–20. *Metropolitan Museum, New York, Wentworth Bequest.*

102 Spice Box, height 2½ ins., by Nicolas Mahon, 1723–24. *Metropolitan Museum, New York, Wentworth Bequest.*

103 Pair of Spice Boxes, 2⅝ ins., by Antoine Filassier, 1723. *Firestone Collection.*

104 Pair of Sugar Casters by Nicolas Besnier, 1728–29. *Metropolitan Museum, New York.*

105 Sugar Bowl, height 5⅝ ins., with Cover and Tray, height ¾ in., by Alexandre de Roussy the Younger. *Metropolitan Museum, New York, Wentworth Bequest.*

106 Sugar Bowl with Cover by Etienne Modenz, 1786–87. *Metropolitan Museum, New York, Wentworth Bequest.*

107, 108 Pair of *Verrières* (monteiths) by Robert-Joseph Auguste, 1782. *M. Stavros Niarchos.*

109 *Verrière*, height 5¼ ins., one of a pair by Henry Auguste, 1789. *Firestone Collection.*

110 Pair of Salad-Oil Bottles. Late seventeenth century. *M. Stavros Niarchos.*

111 *Écuelle.* Paris, 1670. *Firestone Collection.*

112 *Écuelle* by Sébastien Leblond, 1690–92. *Musée du Louvre.*

113 *Écuelle*, length 10⅞ ins., by one of the Fauveau family of Troyes. Early eighteenth century. *Metropolitan Museum, New York, Wentworth Bequest.*

114, 115 Silver-gilt *Écuelle* and Cover by Pierre Jarrin, 1714, with Madrid mark. *M. Stavros Niarchos.*

Preface and Acknowledgements

This book – which seems to be the first of its kind in English – has been made possible by the generous co-operation of the firm of S. J. Phillips which assumed responsibility for the photographs and by the encouragement and expertise of Martin Norton and his son Nicolas. I am hopelessly in debt to them and also to many others, among them Madame Wattel, Mr Marke Zervudachi, M. Jacques Helft, Mr H. S. Tait, Mr Thomas Wragg, Mrs Shirley Bury, Mr Arthur Grimwade, Mr Richard Came, and not forgetting the Trustees of the Wallace Collection, the British Museum, and the Victoria and Albert Museum for granting permission to reproduce. I am also indebted to Presses Universitaires de France for permission to use material from *L'Orfèvrerie Française du XVIIIe Siècle* by Solange Brault and Yves Bottineau; and *L'Orfèvrerie du XIXe Siècle en Europe* by Serge Grandjean, in the appendix. It is scarcely necessary to add that I am deeply grateful to all owners, both public and private, from centres as far apart as Leningrad, Lisbon and Detroit, for permission to publish and that all faults, deficiencies, omissions, errors of judgement and heretical opinions are mine and mine alone.

Early Silver

The ravages of time are as nothing to the greed, folly and lust for destruction of man, that species of the animal kingdom which we flatter by the title of *homo sapiens*. This is not to suggest that every piece of French silver plate was a great masterpiece; merely that where one fine piece of craftsmanship has survived a thousand have perished. One reason is that the metal, whether gold or silver, has an intrinsic value in every age and, until very recently, has been an irresistible temptation in times of economic crisis, whether private or governmental. How often in the past have impoverished monarchs, or impoverished grandees, sent their plate to be melted down so that, while art perished, debts could be paid? For centuries there were only two forms of wealth, land and the precious metals. The former, if one was to lead any kind of existence above starvation level (and not always then) was essential; the latter, as a rule proudly displayed on table or buffet, fashioned into vessels of various shapes, both useful and ornamental, were regarded both as visible signs of the wealth and importance of their owner and as bulwarks against economic disaster. Add to this the theory that bullion not in circulation was inimical to a healthy economy, and remembering the perpetual wars, racial, religious, feudal, dynastic and national, and the marvel is not that so little of the work of generations of gifted craftsmen has survived, but so much. This of course applies not to France alone but to all Europe. Add also the hearty habit, by no means infrequent, of having old-fashioned plate melted down to be refashioned in the latest style and the competent manner in which, during the Revolution, church plate was seized for the benefit of the new-fledged Republic. Those who profess to be shocked by such Gallic excesses can be reminded that a notable precedent had been established two and a half centuries earlier by Henry VIII and his Church Commissioners. Very early (that is, sixteenth century and earlier) French plate exists but appears on the market at such infrequent intervals that the majority of those who take an interest in the subject are liable to ignore it altogether. That two such exceptional pieces as the Burghley Nef on the jacket and Figure 3 and the early sixteenth century table-clock of Figure 1 should have become available during the past ten years – one in 1959, the other in 1968 – is extraordinary.

The Burghley Nef

Nefs are invariably referred to by the French word rather than as ships because they never became fashionable in England. Occasionally they were made for presentation to churches, but normally they were secular objects, used to mark the place of the host at ceremonial banquets and sometimes to do honour to distinguished guests. They were occasionally adapted and presented to churches for use as reliquaries, but, though ex-voto ships are common enough as thank-offerings for a safe return from the perils of the sea, there is little evidence that a goldsmith was ever called upon to provide one. Naturally the normal ex-voto ship would be of wood, but there was one very famous exception – the ship vowed by Queen Marguerite of Provence, wife of St Louis, to the church of Saint Nicolas de Port, near Varangéville in Lorraine, in thanks-giving for the deliverance of herself and her family when in peril during their voyage from Palestine in 1254. When the storm was at its height, says de Joinville, she vowed a ship to the value of five marks of silver and on their safe return 'had the silver ship made in Paris. And there were in the ship the King, the Queen and the three children, all of silver; the sailors, the mast, the tillers and the ropes, all of silver; and the sails all sewn with silver wire. And the Queen told me that the making had cost a hundred livres.' A notable object which appears to have been lost some time in the seventeenth century.

It is difficult to imagine that the Burghley Nef could have been a run-of-the-mill production, for among the few surviving examples it is an object of singular grace, from the elegant mermaid upon which it rests to the crows' nests on two of the three masts. True, the ship is decidedly overgunned and would be liable to capsize in anything but a dead calm, but its maker was not fashioning a dockyard model and was not concerned to provide posterity with an exact replica to scale of a fifteenth century vessel. In one respect it is unique. Seated before the main mast and holding hands over a chess board are two minute little figures, a man and a woman, who can be no other than the love-lorn Tristan and Iseult whiling away the tedium of the voyage from Ireland, already, after drinking the potion, star-crossed and doomed.

Next to nothing is known about its history. The first reference to it is a note added in 1844 to the 1824 inventory of the plate at Burghley House. Its importance was first recognised when Mr Arthur Grimwade made an inventory after the death of the 5th Marquess of Exeter in 1956. It was sold at Christie's in 1959, when the date letter of a crowned

Early Silver

1 Silver-gilt salt, height 13⅜ ins, about 1530

2 Item No 201 in the list of Royal property offered for sale by the Commonwealth, 1649, after the execution of Charles I

3 Detail of the Burghley Nef illustrated on the jacket

4 Above : Silver and enamel bowl, diameter 17 cm, Paris, 1450
5 Left : Detail.   The dark portion is enamel
6 Right : Unidentified mark

7 Bowl with unidentified coat of arms, c 1480

8 Shallow silver bowl, plain boss in centre
9 Unidentified mark

10 Silver-gilt cup with handle (cover missing), late 15th century

10A Two rock-crystal and silver-gilt pricket candlesticks, late 16th century

11 Silver ewer, maker's mark D F and bird, Paris, 1603-4

12 Ewer, Paris, late 17th century

13 Parcel-gilt cup, 5¼ ins high, Orleans, mid-16th century

14 Silver-gilt and chased standing cup and cover, no marks, c 1550

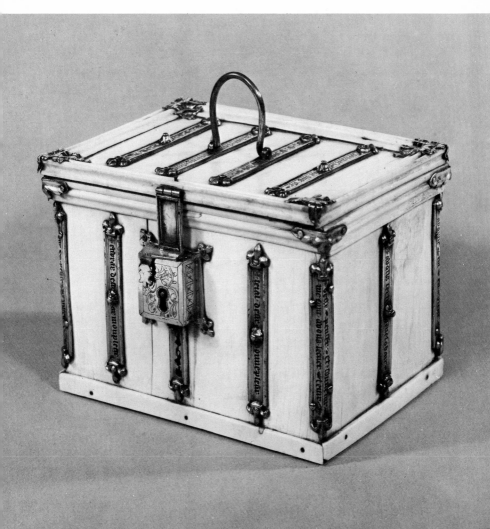

15 Ivory casket with silver-gilt bands, length 6 ins, 16th century

16 Silver-gilt standing cup with map prepared by Oronce Finé, no marks, 16th century

Y was thought to indicate the year 1505. But the maker, Pierre le Flamand – his mark is a *fleur-de-lis courronée et au-dessous deux bannières en croix de St André* – is first mentioned in 1462. As Mr Charles Oman points out in his Victoria and Albert Monograph *Mediaeval Silver Nefs*, 'This (a date of 1505) would mean that Pierre le Flamand had an unusually long working life, and there appears to be no real objection to the attribution of this date-letter (otherwise unknown) to the previous cycle and the year 1482'. He was apparently in full activity at this period and served as Warden of the Paris Guild in 1478, 1483 and 1489. An interesting point about the two figures of Tristan and Iseult is that they are wearing clothes of about a century earlier. Oman suggests that they were cast from a model which had been lying about in the workshop for a very long time and also that this romantic subject must have been used on many occasions before.

Silver-gilt Salt

This magnificent enamel and silver-gilt salt, Figure 1, is a rediscovery of more than ordinary importance. Enriched with cameo busts and semi-precious stones, it has been accepted by all authorities as of French workmanship and by the same hand as a small box in the Cathedral in Mantua which bears the Paris mark for 1532-3, maker's mark B. The same unknown maker was also responsible for a celebrated ciborium in the Louvre. But the salt, which now belongs to the Worshipful Company of Goldsmiths, has yet another claim to our attention. Until it appeared at Christie's in July 1967 only two items from the Royal Tudor Inventories had been identified, one of them the fourteenth century gold and enamel cup (also French) in the British Museum, and a gold and enamel mounted crystal bowl in the Schatzkammer, Munich. The salt, which originally contained a clock, and whose cover was decorated with agate heads and emeralds with a man seated upon a bird as a finial, is first identifiable in the inventory of 'The Kinges Juelhous' in 1550, and again in that of 1574. It next appears as No. 201 in the list of objects belonging to the King sold by the Commonwealth in 1649 after the execution of Charles I (Figure 2). There were evidently two, valued together at £40, and sold in December of that year for £43 to a Mr Smith. Nothing more was heard of the salt (and nothing whatever of a pair – a second has not come to light) until 1862 when it was exhibited at South Kensington. It was there described as French, *circa* 1520, and was lent by Mr W. B. Stopford, grandfather of Colonel Nigel Stopford Sackville who sold it at Christie's.

Now that its resemblance to the box at Mantua and to the ciborium at the Louvre has been recognised, it is tempting to regard it as a gift from Francis I to his brother monarch Henry VIII. If, as seems more than likely, it was a royal commission, the maker, the unknown B, would not have to send it for marking, as he did in the case of the box at Mantua which was presumably made for a less exalted patron. It is, in any case, a Renaissance piece of the greatest interest and beauty and it is pleasant to be able to illustrate it here as something of French workmanship which once belonged to the Tudor Monarchy and which remains in safe hands in England.

Styles in Early French Silver

The three bowls, Figures 4, 7 and 8, are all from the second half of the fifteenth century : the earliest, by perhaps a few years, is Figure 4 with an unidentified Paris mark. Figure 7, the coat of arms in the centre unidentified, is in the David Weill Collection in the Louvre, its date about 1480, while the third bowl, a shallow vessel with a plain boss in the centre, Figure 8, is in the British Museum. This is said to have been found in the bed of the Rhine and also has an unidentified mark (Figure 9). Figure 10, also from the late fifteenth century, is a cup with a flat curved handle with rolled-over end and engraved; the cover is missing; this is part of the Franks Bequest at the British Museum.

Styles in silver as in all the arts change slowly, the new ideas generally initiated in the capital city, which is almost inevitably the centre of patronage, and gradually penetrating into the provinces. The time lag, when communications are slow and local taste conservative, can be considerable, not just one or two years – the time it takes for Paris rag-trade fashions to reach Wigan – but one or two decades.

The sophistication and elegance achieved in Paris during the second half of the sixteenth century are beautifully illustrated by the two rock-crystal and silver-gilt pricket candlesticks of Figure 10A, recently brought back to England from the United States where they appear to have been since 1925. They are recorded by Rosenburg under the section devoted to the Treasury of the Chapelle du Saint-Esprit, Paris; maker's mark, an elephant with a crowned fleur-de-lis above, crescent below. The date is 1583-4. Each candlestick is raised on four supports formed as cherub heads, their stretched wings pinned back above their heads. The stems are formed of panels of faceted rock-crystal with octagonal knops, the wide wax pans chased to match the base; a rock-crystal knop is missing from each candlestick below the wax-pan. They were formerly in the W. F. Cook Collection, numbers 230-31 in the 1904 catalogue, and were sold in the Humphrey W. Cook sale at Christie's on 7 July,

1925. A somewhat similar pair still remains in the Chapelle du Saint-Esprit.

Perhaps the change in style between the early and later years of the seventeenth century can be seen most clearly by a close look at the two splendid ewers of Figures 11 and 12. They come almost from different worlds. The former, with its rectangular handle terminating below in a three-quarter ring, sparse band of formal engraving round the body and square engraved thumbpiece, looks back far into the mediaeval past, the present indicated by the chased ornament round the foot. The date is 1603-4, the maker an unknown whose mark was D. F. and a bird – Paris work, which is now in the Musée des Arts Decoratifs. Figure 12, the helmet-shaped ewer with the eagle-head handle, is a typical and magnificent example of the style in favour from about 1650 until the end of the century.

The cup of Figure 13, in the Victoria and Albert Museum, is probably half a century earlier than the ewer of Figure 11. This also looks back as well as forward and is besides a notable survival of provincial workmanship – in this case from Orleans.

Mid-sixteenth century ingenuity at its most elaborate and, many will add with a smile, mid-sixteenth century taste at its most Victorian, is beautifully displayed by the standing cup and cover, silver-gilt and chased, and covered with cameos on shells – seven on the cover, ten on the body, five on the foot – from the Waddesdon Bequest at the British Museum (the figure which surmounts it is inappropriate and nineteenth century) (Figure 14). The small ivory casket – six inches long – enriched with silver-gilt bands is from the same bequest (Figure 15), while the standing globe cup of Figure 16 and the nef of Figure 17 are from the Franks Bequest.

The cup, its globe presumably supported by Atlas, bears eloquent witness to the widening of man's horizons by the sixteenth century explorers. There is no mark, but the map was prepared by Oronce Finé; the land masses are gilt, the oceans silver. The nef bears no mark, nor any indication of origin, but is thought to be French of about 1530 and possibly from some centre in the Rhône Valley. It is as light-hearted (and as unseaworthy) a vessel as ever existed, fit for any royal table of that time – Francis I would be a suitable candidate – and could well be regarded as a major enchantment among the few surviving nefs in the world were it not for the existence of the earlier vessel of 1482 illustrated in the frontispiece, which, I imagine most readers will agree, is very greatly its superior.

With the silver-gilt pilgrim bottle of Figure 18 we are almost in another dimension – a world in which beauty is dependent upon smooth surfaces and harmonious balance rather than upon intricate ornament.

Seeing this for the first time one might be forgiven perhaps for venturing to suggest a date of about 1700 though a closer look at the climbing dragons at each side to which the chains are attached would soon put one on the right track. The point is, of course, that the shape remained constant for many years, and not only in France. This is silver-gilt and is engraved with the arms of Henri III, King of France and of Poland, encircled by the collar of the Order of the St Esprit. It is in the Louvre, attributed to the hand of Noël Delacroix, probably 1581-2.

The ewer and dish (Figure 19), since the above was written, has been on the market in Paris and is now, at any rate for the moment, in London. The maker is Louis Regnard, the year 1747, and it takes its place here not merely as a fine thing of its kind but as showing how the tradition of the distant past could still exercise the imagination of a first class silversmith at the height of the fashion for rococo; even during the liveliest years of the mid-eighteenth century, it was still tempting to look back over one's shoulder and adapt old ideals to new practice.

The most famous of all early French vessels in England, the Royal Gold and Enamel Cup in the British Museum, has been deliberately omitted from this survey. It would be impossible to convey any notion of its quality except in full colour. It must suffice to note that it is of Paris workmanship and was presented in 1391 by the Duc de Berry to his nephew King Charles VI of France.

The Gold Plate of Anne of Austria

The casket and the beaker of the illustrations are each of gold, not silver-gilt, and are believed to have belonged to Anne of Austria (1601-1666) wife of Louis XIII, mother of Louis XIV and Regent of France during the latter's minority. She was the daughter of Philip III of Spain and was never popular in France, partly because the claustrophobic etiquette of the Spanish court in which she had been brought up was a poor training ground for a less inhibited country, partly because, after the death of the king, she depended overmuch upon the advice of her chief minister, Cardinal Mazarin. These two superb objects appear to be the sole survivors of a great quantity of gold plate, for among the list of her possessions at her death was a toilet set in gold, not less than twelve plates, a covered cup, a sugar bowl, a cruet, a cadenas and three covers, each composed of a spoon, a fork and a knife, the whole weighing more than twelve kilograms. In this seeming extravagance she was merely continuing an ancient and honourable tradition for, in the fourteenth century, the gold plate belonging to Charles v consisted, according to the inventories, of two hundred and twenty-four pieces. Her son Louis XIV inherited her collection and added to it.

The casket (Figure 20), which bears no mark, but can be dated to about 1645, is *repoussé*, chased and pierced on a wooden ground covered in blue silk, in an intricate design of flowers and foliage. Tradition, which is long established and not to be wholly disregarded, records that it was a present to the Queen from the Cardinal, who lived in princely fashion and introduced to a comparatively backward court all the refinements of his native Italy. It is in any case a masterpiece of its kind and must have been the work of a craftsman of exceptional ability – possibly someone from beyond the borders of France, for then, as a century later, Paris attracted Europe's best workers. Somehow the casket escaped the melting pot in 1689 (the first financial crisis during the reign of Louis XIV) and again in 1709 (the second). It is heard of again at the Restoration after the fall of Napoleon, when it was placed in the king's bedroom in the Tuileries and then, during the reign of Louis Philippe, in one of the reception rooms. It is now in the Louvre. The beaker (Figure 21), once in the Puiforcat collection and now, through the generosity of Mr Stavros Niarchos, destined with the other pieces from that superb accumulation of French silver also to belong to the nation, has a later inscription on the foot 'Gobelet d'Anne d'Autriche – 1601-1666 – Liancourt'. The Château of Liancourt was the home of Anne Gabory, one of the Queen's ladies-in-waiting, and there is no reason to doubt that it was a present from Anne of Austria. No less than the casket it is an object of singular beauty, its elegant spiral ribs enriched in the hollows by engraved flowers and foliage. It was a pleasure both to see and to handle; as with so many other intimate, small objects from the past, he is a dull dog who, holding such a thing in his hands, fails to visualise the hopes and fears, the responsibilities, the inevitable disappointments of its original widowed owner.

An Inkstand of 1670

As a contrast to the sophistication of the great majority of the objects illustrated in this survey, this inkstand (Figure 22) in its slightly gawky simplicity, can scarcely be bettered. It is by some unknown silversmith of Avignon, its date about 1670, length 6⅝ inches, weight 22 ozs, 14 dwts. By Paris standards of that decade, when the power and prestige of Louis XIV were at their height and the disasters of the later years of his reign were unimaginable, it would probably have been dismissed as drearily provincial; nor, one can suppose, would the great silversmiths of the following century have done more than display it to their pupils and patrons as the kind of primitive structure, all rectangles and smooth surfaces, which the march of progress had rendered hopelessly old-fashioned. The modern world, perhaps less sure of itself and certainly more sympathetic to every kind of experiment in the arts, takes a very different view, and holds these simple designs by unknown men, wherever made, in no less honour than the most elaborate masterpieces by Germain or Roëttiers.

Three Beakers

While the gold beaker of Anne of Austria (Figure 21) clearly remains in a class by itself, these three display at one and the same time the intense conservatism of the French tradition and its capacity to absorb new ideas. It is more than likely that when the beaker now in the Hermitage at Leningrad (Figure 23), by some unknown Paris silversmith, was first seen in 1731-2, many possible purchasers, not yet accustomed to this fluid asymmetrical style – in spite of all the talk about a fresh attitude to art, away with solemnity and the dreary traditions of the reign of Louis xiv and whatever was then the slang for being with-it and trendy – found themselves at odds with the world and longed for the more decorous past. If they did, they would not have far to go, nor would they have to wait long, for throughout the 1730's and well into the 1750's, in spite of fashion and the example of the king himself (melting down the royal plate and having it rehashed), the old order, though submerged in high quarters, was by no means destroyed. Here are two which provide ample evidence that past ideals could still find favour. The first is a beaker of 1737 by François Balzac (Figure 25), the second is the admirable example of Strasbourg craftsmanship in the Victoria and Albert Museum by Jean Stahl, 1754 – by which time the rococo revolution was at its height (Figure 26). Yet each beaker, were it not for the irrefutable evidence of the date letter, could easily have been made about half a century earlier.

Cadenas by Henry Auguste
(1759-1816, Master 1785)

Cadenas, or ceremonial platter, was a royal prerogative from the time of Charles v which, in those days, would be accompanied by a nef. This one (Figure 28), was part of the elaborate service presented to Napoleon by the City of Paris and used at a banquet given for him in the Hôtel de Ville on 5 December 1804, three days after his coronation. It was made for the Empress Josephine, a variant of the one made for Napoleon himself, and has found a final and appropriate resting place in the Musée de Malmaison, the charming little château near Paris to which Josephine retired and where she died and which is now restored and refurnished much as she knew it. The service continued to be used after the fall of Napoleon but the decorative insignia on the cadenas were changed on two occasions, first by the restored Bourbons when the Bonaparte bees which form a diaper pattern in the centre were replaced by fleurs-de-lis, and secondly by Napoleon III who substituted reproductions of the original bees. Upon the cadenas were placed bread, knife, fork and spoon, covered with the royal napkin. At the further end a small coffer contained salt, pepper and spices traditionally fastened with a padlock (*cadenas*) as a protection against poisoning. Length 14¼ inches. Silver-gilt. In addition to the inscription Hy. Auguste this piece bears a post-Revolution maker's mark – i.e. H.A. with a spear between a wolf's head above, a bear's head below, in a lozenge (Figure 29).

Other pieces of this sumptuous service have the maker's mark of before the Revolution – a crowned fleur-de-lis, two grains, crossed palm branches and H. A. beneath; the Wardens' mark for 1789-90 – a crowned P with 89; the charge mark for 1789-92, an A with an indecipherable figure, in a circle with latticed border, and the unofficial Assay mark for 1793-4 – a head of Apollo with P in an oval. The Napoleonic insignia would have been added for the occasion.

Nécessaire de Voyage

When the travelling case of the illustration (Figure 30) was first filled with the various objects considered necessary for the comfort of the Queen of France, Marie-Antoinette, it contained not less than one hundred and seventeen pieces ranging from knives and forks, teapots and *écuelles* to writing and sewing utensils. It is now in the Louvre and still holds ninety-six of its original contents. According to Madame Campan in her Memoirs, the Queen, in making preparations for the flight of the Royal Family which ended so disastrously at Varennes, thought of sending this fitted travelling case in advance to her sister Marie-Christine, Duchess of Saxe-Teschen and Regent of the Low Countries. But she decided this might arouse suspicion and so asked the chargé d'affaires of the Emperor of Austria in Paris to order, on behalf of Marie-Christine, a travelling case similar to her own. This was put in hand immediately, and meanwhile Marie-Antoinette sent her own case to her sister in Brussels. When, after the Revolution, the French invaded the Low Countries in 1792, the case was taken to Italy (some of its contents bear the additional Milan mark for 1794) and the Archduke Ferdinand, the Queen's brother, presented it to Count Terzi of Bergamo. Bergamo was captured by the French during the campaign in Italy which established young General Napoleon's reputation, and he offered the case to Josephine. It was however finally, in 1805, sold to Felice Origoni, whose descendants kept it until the last war. The second fitted case which the Queen ordered and which remained in France was almost certainly melted down in 1795. The box of mahogany was made by Palma, who described himself as *'ébéniste et faiseur de nécessaires'*, 34 Vieille Rue du Temple en face du Palais Cardinal. Out of the ninety-six pieces it still contains, twenty-six are of silver, the majority by Jean-Pierre Charpenat; thirty-seven are of crystal (the flasks silver-mounted), eleven of porcelain, fifteen of ivory, seven of other materials. The porcelain is from the little factory in the Rue Thiroux, Paris, which was started in 1775 (perhaps a little earlier) by Leboeuf under the patronage of the Queen. Its productions during her lifetime were known as *'Porcelaine de la Reine'*.

The word *nécessaire* seems to have been used with this specialised meaning for the first time on 24 March 1718 in a letter written by the Dowager Duchesse d'Orléans in which she says, 'My son has given his sister a *nécessaire*; it is a little square box in which is everything one needs for tea, coffee, chocolate. The cups are white, everything else gold and enamel.' Throughout the eighteenth century *nécessaires* were made in great numbers. During the reign of Louis xv Lazare Duvaux often uses the word in his ledger; on 24 December 1752, for instance, he supplies the king with one contained in a lacquer casket with compartments lined with moiré silk, the cups, etc., of porcelain and spoons of gold. In addition to the one illustrated, the Louvre (thanks to the Society of the Friends of the Louvre and to Mr Stavros Niarchos) also owns the celebrated *nécessaire* by Henry-Nicolas Cousinet (1729-1730) which was presented to Queen Marie Leczinska, probably by Louis xv to celebrate the birth of the Dauphin in that year. This is no doubt the one described in the inventory made at Versailles after the Queen's death: 'A *nécessaire* in palisander wood, furnished entirely with porcelain and silver-gilt.'

A Basin and Casket at Munich

When Max Emanuel was driven from his inheritance in 1704 during the war of the Spanish Succession, he fled to France and, as a faithful client who had suffered in the cause of righteousness – that is, in support of French policy – was welcomed by Louis xiv and provided with a more than adequate income – sufficient for him to build a fine château at St Cloud, entertain lavishly, keep an extravagant mistress, patronise Charles-André Boulle for furniture, and numerous Paris jewellers and

17 Silver-gilt Nef,
no marks, prob-
ably French,
c 1530

18 Silver-gilt bottle, height 12 ins, attributed Noël Delacroix, 1581-2
19 Opposite : Ewer and dish by Louis Regnard, 1747

20 Gold casket, no marks, c 1645

21 Gold beaker, 1st half 17th century
22 Inkstand, length 6⅝ ins, weight 22
oz 14 dwts, Avignon, c 1670

24 Base of beaker in figure 23

25 Beaker by François Balzac,
Paris, 1737

26 Silver-gilt beaker by Jean Stahl, Strasbourg, 1754
27 Mark on the beaker

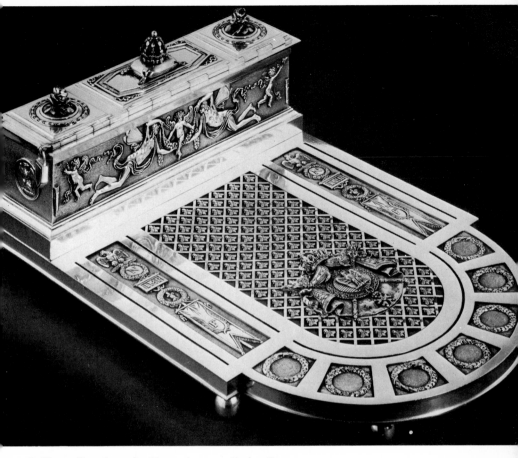

28 Silver-gilt cadenas by Henry Auguste, Paris, 1804
29 Mark on the cadenas

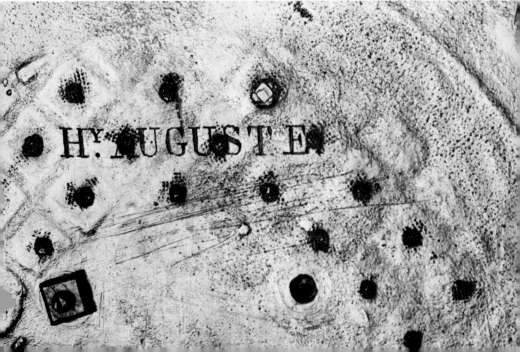

30 Marie-Antoinette's *Nécessaire de Voyage*, case of mahogany, contents of silver, porcelain and ivory

31 Basin by Claude II Ballin, 1712-13
32 Marks on basin

33 Casket by Claude II Ballin,
1712-13
34 Mark on casket

silversmiths. Among his purchases was a clock, silver and part-gilt, enriched with enamel, diamonds and rubies with a bas-relief in gold commemorating his prowess when he was an ally of Austria against the Turks, and also the basin (Figure 31) and casket (Figure 33) of the illustrations, each of them by Claude II Ballin (Master 1688. Died 1754, aged 93, thus living even longer than his younger and brilliant contemporary in the furniture world, the great Boulle). Both pieces are dated 1712-13, and are preserved with many of Max Emanuel's other possessions in the Residenz Museum at Munich. Though they come from the last years of the reign of Louis XIV, their style remains essentially that of the previous century, monumental and dignified, related to the designs for the royal plate executed by Nicolas Delaunay and preserved in the National Museum at Stockholm. The plate itself was spared in 1709 when so much went to the melting pot (after it had been decided that 'the royal family should be served on silver and silver-gilt, the princes and princesses of the blood on faïence') but did not escape when Louis XV found it old fashioned and had it melted down to provide the metal for new pieces more à la mode.

Each of these pieces by Ballin is a supremely good example of its kind, with their contrasting areas of smooth and decorated surfaces. It has been suggested that the basin was used as a bottle stand with or without ice, the casket possibly for knives or other adjuncts of the table.

A Rock-Crystal Ewer
and Basin Mounted in Gold

Most visitors to the Wallace Collection enter Hertford House to see furniture or paintings or both. A few become obsessed by the arms and armour, fewer still by the smaller, more modest objects which are to be found in that astonishing place. Not many of us, until Anthony Radcliffe drew our attention to it in his *European Bronze Statuettes*, had given much more than a glance at one of the most enchanting little bronzes of the Renaissance, an eight-inch high, seated nymph by a certain Giovanni Fonduli de Crema who was working in Padua during the second half of the fifteenth century – nor, I imagine, have many paused to look carefully at the gold-mounted rock-crystal ewer and basin of the illustration (Figures 35 and 36). The mark (Figure 37, A and B) is that of the tax-farmer Cottin, 1727-1732, but the actual date-letter has been defaced. (The Louvre possesses a smilar ewer and basin of a slightly simpler design which belonged to Queen Marie Antoinette.) As the inventory of the estate of Madame de Pompadour, drawn up after her death in 1764, mentions several gold-mounted objects of this sort, it is quite possible that the Wallace Collection ewer also belonged to her. It is in any case a superb example of its kind, with a little dog as the lid finial and a child struggling with a dragon for handle. The anonymous goldsmith has echoed the flowing curves of the ewer with apparently carefree exuberance – exuberance which is in fact most cunningly contrived.

There is, of course, nothing out of the way in this treatment of hard-stones. Gold mounts are inevitably rare, but there were few things a silversmith enjoyed more than ornamenting porphyry or jasper vases or something equally precious with gold or silver-gilt, a fashion brought to the highest possible perfection by the workers in ormolu (gilded bronze) who arranged some astonishingly successful marriages between Chinese porcelain (particularly celadon, whose olive-green harmonised so happily with the pulsating dull sheen of the gilded bronze) and with the porcelains from Meissen and Sèvres. There is a famous ewer of jasper in the Gulbenkian Foundation in Lisbon, less playful, more majestic than this rock-crystal example, but with certain affinities. The vessel itself is possibly of Byzantine workmanship and many centuries older than the mount, which is also of gold. Its handle in its upper part is formed as a goat while a small child surmounts the lid, a design taken from an illustration in the *Book of Vases* by Boucher, published in 1734. An older and more famous piece is the eagle of the great ecclesiastic and statesman Suger, the body a vase of porphyry with wings and head of silver-gilt which dates from the middle of the twelfth century.

This method of enriching objects which were rarities in their own right is of great antiquity and was in no way confined to France. But the French royal house owned many exquisite things of the kind, a great number of which – some collected by the Valois, some by Cardinal Mazarin, others by Louis xiv and by his son, Le Grand Dauphin, who predeceased him – have survived and are in the Louvre. While some seem to be of German or Italian origin, others are French, among them a small sardonyx bowl mounted in gold, its date about 1685, which has been identified as one of the items in a royal inventory of the period. The immense riches of the French crown in this category alone in the second half of the seventeenth century can be gauged by the fact that when the Dauphin died, a part of his collection went to Philip v of Spain, and one hundred and twenty pieces from this inheritance are now in the Prado. Others, a few of which are in the Louvre, were sold to pay the dead prince's debts, and it is thought that some of them were bought by his father. Saint-Simon, as usual, commented sharply upon this dispersal, noting how the courtiers were able to enter the apartment of the widow at Marly laughing, gossiping and looking for bargains.

Les Toilettes

The fame of the Sun King and all his works was prodigious. Every princeling of Europe basked in the warm rays which shone forth from Versailles and nourished the hope that he too might some day attain to the sophistication, if not the wealth, of that highly civilised monarch.* French fashions, then as now, were no less à la mode in London, partly on their own merits, partly perhaps because the susceptible Charles II was fond of his sister, Minette, married to the Dauphin, and was enamoured of Louise de Kéroualle, whom he created Duchess of Portsmouth and, it is not unreasonable to assume, further favourably disposed to all things French, by a secret and most welcome pension of £200,000 per annum from Louis. Charles presented a superb toilet service to Frances Stuart, 'La belle Stuart', Duchess of Richmond (Paris 1672-7) which is now in the Edinburgh Museum.

The other great seventeenth century toilet service in the British Isles belongs to the Duke of Devonshire at Chatsworth (Figures 38, 39 and 40), a dignified and richly decorated ensemble in the tradition of some twenty or thirty years earlier rather than in the slightly more exuberant manner of the year it was made. Its author is Pierre Prévost, the date 1670-1. It bears the arms and cypher of Mary, daughter of James II, together with those of her husband William of Orange whom she married in 1677; arms and cypher were no doubt added in that year. As in all other toilet services until well into the nineteenth century the principal piece is the mirror; there are various flasks and boxes, ewer and basin, candlesticks, while the long tray in the middle row is for the snuffers next to it. Two unexpected items amid these luxurious silver-gilt adjuncts to beauty are (Figure 38, top left) the small *écuelle*, the charming little covered bowl which was a familiar table utensil from this time onwards, and the covered vase with the handle on the extreme right; apparently each was a normal item in the great toilet sets of the period. The casket (bottom centre) has a pin cushion inserted in the lid.

* I use the word 'civilised' with diffidence, for when Louis exclaimed: 'Away with those monstrosities!' he was referring to Notre-Dame.

The original owner was destined to share the throne of England with her husband.

Two silver-gilt flasks from the same period (1669-70) belonging to the Victoria and Albert Museum and evidently part of a service of equal splendour are also illustrated (Figures 41 and 42) – the maker PDN has not been identified.

The silver-gilt oval basin from the Louvre is all that remains from what was evidently a noble service almost certainly executed by Nicolas Besnier for the Duchesse d'Orléans between 1717 and 1722 (Figure 43). This is such an elegantly proportioned vessel that anyone might be forgiven for thinking, at first sight, that it might be by some hitherto great unknown from late in the eighteenth century – someone who had absorbed the spirit of neo-classicism while still clinging to the dignified ideals of the early years of the French Regency. Every sensitive visitor who has seen this basin in the Louvre has been spellbound by its subtle harmonies – by the flowing scroll work, the shell motif in the centre, the smooth boat-shaped curve of the lower portion – all these contrasting with the children's heads at each end, chubby-faced infants apparently about to extinguish a candle on a birthday cake (they presumably symbolise Zephyr or Boreas). There is of course no question about the date and very little about the maker, for this reason: the vessel bears the arms of the Duchesse d'Orléans, legitimate daughter of Louis xiv and of Madame de Montespan, who was known as Mademoiselle de Blois before her marriage in 1692 to the Duc de Chartres, the future Duc d'Orléans and, after the death of Louis xiv in 1715, Regent of France until the accession of the late King's great-grandson, Louis xv. In 1722, Nicolas Besnier delivered a basin for the toilet service destined for the Spanish fiancée of Louis xv; the description of this basin in the *Journal du Garde-Meuble* could well have been that of the one illustrated. According to an inventory of 1724-5, the Duchess evidently kept this basin, together with the service of which it was a part, in her apartment at Versailles. When she died in 1749 the whole service, in accordance with normal court usage, passed to her lady-in-waiting, the Duchesse de Lorges. The tradition was long-lived, providing notable opportunities for the finest craftsmen of the day to exercise their skill.

Two other services give an indication of their quality, and of how to live in princely fashion provided one has plenty of servants expert in polishing. The first is from the hands of four makers, Sebastien Igonet, Alexis Loir iii, Antoine Lebrun, and Etienne Pollet, the date 1738-9 (Figure 44). It was commisioned by Don Jaime, 3rd Duc de Cadaval, whose arms it bears, when he married the daughter of the Prince de Lambèse. Saint-Simon refers to the Cadaval family as 'les plus grands seigneurs' of Portugal, which accounts for the quality of these pieces which can compare with any toilet service made for royalty. A few objects normally in such services are missing – the tray for gloves, for instance, and the flasks for perfume. While it was not unknown for silversmiths to combine together for a special commission, the four men who provided this sumptuous service do not seem to have been particularly well known at the time, and there has been a good deal of speculation as to why a grandee of the calibre of Cadaval should have chosen them. The query is perhaps academic – who really cares who the makers were? – but at least it draws attention to the undoubted fact that there were other fine craftsmen besides the admittedly great Thomas Germain. It has been suggested however that as Thomas Germain was the Paris silversmith who enjoyed the favour of the Portuguese Court until his death in 1748, this exceptionally beautiful set may well have been made under his direction by others because he himself was too occupied with royal commissions.

With the remaining toilet service we are well into the second half of the eighteenth century, 1765-6, one of the many commissions carried out by François-Thomas Germain for the Empress Catherine, and one of the many treasures of the Hermitage, Leningrad (Figures 45 and 46). F.-T. Germain became bankrupt in 1765 and was succeeded in royal favour by the Roëttiers, father and son.

The curious refinement of a special tray for gloves (*une gantière*) is illustrated here by a lovely example from the Catherine D. Wentworth Bequest to the Metropolitan Museum, New York (Figure 47). This seems also a suitable point at which to illustrate three ewers and basins, each presumably from some majestic toilet service, the earliest 1727-9, the second some ten years or so later, the third from well into the nineteenth century. The first is by Léopold Antoine (Figure 48) who registered his name in the Guild book in 1706 and who is last recorded as working in 1729, the second (Figure 51), very similar in style though not in detail, is by Jean Fauche, who was Master in 1733 and died in 1762; both of them are from the same bequest to the Metropolitan. The third, once in the Puiforcat Collection and now in that of Mr Niarchos (Figures 49 and 50), is a characteristic work of the years 1809-19.

The nine-inch wide casket (Figure 52) is presumably – though not necessarily – part of a toilet service, and a beautiful example of the work of Nicolas Besnier, 1714, whose daughter married the elder Roëttiers, so that one can say that grandfather, son-in-law and grandson made as notable a contribution to their craft during the eighteenth century as did the two Germains, father and son.

The little globe-shaped soap box (Figure 53) apparently bears the date letter for 1729 and the mark of Pierre Prévost who was responsible for the great service at Chatsworth of 1670-1. It used to be considered that his last recorded work was in 1716; if the mark on the soap box is correctly deciphered, Prévost enjoyed a working life well beyond the normal span. A second soap box (Figure 54), by a less well-known silversmith, Pierre Hannier, 1730, its cover and the upper part of the body pierced with quatrefoils and scrolling foliage, is illustrated next to it.

Since the above was written, the ewer and basin (Figure 55) have been seen at Christie's – a fine example by Sebastien Igonet, 1733, one of the collaborators in the service made for the Duke of Cadaval (Figure 44).

Pieces for the Dining Table

Not everything which makes auction-room history (so unpredictable are the changes in fashion), is necessarily the finest thing of its kind. One cannot though go very far wrong in expressing the opinion that, whatever elaborate silver services were made for greater grandees by other silversmiths of the day, that fashioned by Jacques Roëttiers during the three years 1735-7 for Augustus, the 4th Earl of Berkeley, is as fine as any (Figures 56-61). James, the 3rd Earl, died in 1736 at the château of his father-in-law, the Duke of Richmond, at Aubigny in France. He had married in 1710 Louise, daughter of Charles Lennox, 1st Duke of Richmond, son of Charles II by the Duchess of Portsmouth who was also, in her native country, Duchesse d'Aubigny. The son, Augustus, would have come of age in 1737 and it is thought that the service may have been begun for the coming-of-age celebrations and added to the following year. The service remained at Berkeley Castle (as remarkable a family residence as exists anywhere in England) from the moment it was delivered and apparently was not regarded as anything very much out of the ordinary though it was laid out on a table and shown to visitors when, after the last war, the place was opened to the public. All the pieces are engraved with the arms of Berkeley. It was recognised as of exceptional importance as the result of a fortuitous visit Mr Martin Norton paid to Berkeley Castle soon afterwards.

The maker's family, as the name indicates, was of Flemish origin. Jacques Roëttiers' father was engraver to the Paris Mint (he had previously done similar work in London) and because of this his son was able, after learning his craft from the elder Germain and from Besnier, to register his mark in 1733 without having to undergo a formal apprenticeship. In 1734 Jacques married Besnier's daughter and in 1737 was given one of the lucrative Royal appointments. He was able to retire in 1772, to be followed by his son Jacques-Nicolas Roëttiers, who registered his mark in 1765, and we hear no more of him after 1777; but it was he who was responsible for the enormous service commissioned by Catherine the Great for her favourite, Prince Orloff. The latter was supplanted by Potemkine in 1773 and died mad ten years later. Meanwhile he had cost Russia a prodigious amount of treasure. Originally this Orloff service consisted of eight hundred and forty-two pieces. The Empress bought it back from his heirs. The greater part remains at the Kremlin and the Hermitage, but between the two wars the USSR sold pieces, some of which are in private collections, others in American museums, in the Louvre and a few in the Nissim de Camondo Museum.

The Berkeley service was seen in public at Sotheby's on 16 June 1960 and was, very boldly, offered as a single lot. Within five minutes it had been sold for the formidable sum – or what seemed then the formidable sum – of £207,000, and so went to join the other magnificent pieces of French plate already in the Niarchos collection, chiefly the Puiforcat silver which Mr Niarchos acquired before its dispersal in Paris, arranging that, after his death and that of his son it should go to the Louvre.

It is a little difficult for twentieth century man to realise how readily these great services were taken for granted, particularly during the eighteenth century. In spite of recurring financial crises the extravagance of Versailles was endemic, and what the monarch considered necessary for his comfort and dignity was, on the whole, not very much above the ambitions if not the resources of lesser men. While Louis xiv was compelled to consign much of his own silver to the melting pot and to order the court to do likewise, he could not bring himself to discard immediately the prodigious amount of gold pieces, some of which he had inherited, others which he had acquired from time to time – a great gold nef, for instance, in 1671, and a cadenas executed by Delaunay in 1678. Apart from the various dishes, plates, etc., the King also owned sixty-eight *étuis*, each containing knife, fork and spoon, also in gold : but nearly all this was melted down during the final years of his reign.

Louis xv, having announced that he wished to be served at table in no less handsome a manner than his grandfather, proceeded to replace much of what had been lost. Once again Delaunay was commissioned – in 1724 he deivered a two kilogram cadenas, three years later a second even heavier, an oil and vinegar cruet, a salt and pepper in one, thirty plates, two dozen spoons, forks and knife handles. Delaunay was succeeded by Thomas Germain, who provided a gold spoon for olives in 1728, an *écuelle* in 1736, and a famous pair of girandoles in 1747. After Germain's death in 1748, Jacques Roëttiers provided yet more plates, etc., of gold and the sugar vases (which were placed in the King's bedchamber at Versailles) decorated with *bas-reliefs* with a design of little negroes working in a sugar factory. By the end of his reign, in addition to the exceptional rarities just mentioned, Louis xv owned fifty-two gold plates and three dozen complete *couverts* (plate, knife, fork and spoon). Lesser mortals had to be content with silver or silver-gilt, though a few specially favoured persons owned some very choice objects in

35 Gold-mounted rock-crystal ewer and basin, height 18.4 cm, maker unknown, 1727-32

36 Detail of gold
handle and cover
of figure 35
37 A and B Marks
on ewer

38 The Chatsworth toilet service by Pierre Prévost, 1670-1

39 A Box from the
Chatsworth toilet service
40 Mark of Pierre Prévost on
the Chatsworth box

41 Pair of silver-gilt flasks
maker's mark PDN with a fleur
de lis, height 6⅞ ins, Paris,
1669-70
42 Mark on flask

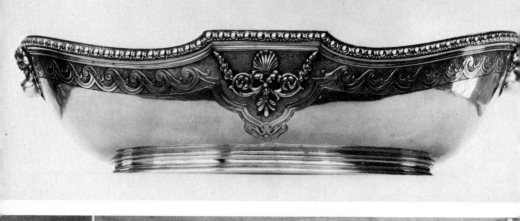

43 Silver-gilt basin, 34 cm, attributed to Nicolas Besnier, 1717-22

44 Toilet service by Sébastien Igonet, Alexis Loir III, Antoine Lebrun and
Etienne Pollet, Paris, 1738-39

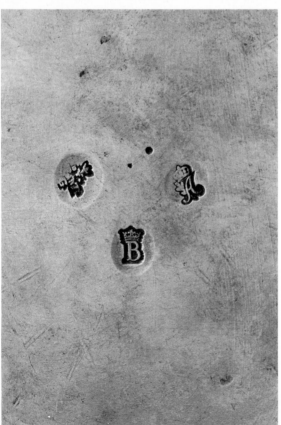

45 Toilet service by François-
Thomas Germain, 1765
46 Mark on toilet service

47 Glove tray, height 1⅝ ins, 18th century
48 Ewer and basin by Léopold Antoine, Paris, 1727-29

49 Silver-gilt ewer and basin,
Paris, 1809-19
50 Ewer and basin mark

51 Ewer and basin by Jean Fauche, Paris, 1739-42
52 Box, height 3¾ ins, by Nicolas Besnier, 1714

53 Soap box, height 3 ins, by Pierre Prévost, 1729

54 Soap box by Pierre Hannier, 1730

55 Ewer and basin, height 9½ ins, by Sébastien Igonet, 1733

Pieces for the Dining Table

56 Terrine, one of a
pair from the Berkeley
Castle Service by Jacques
Roëttiers, 1737
57 Detail of cover

58 Cover from a second pair of terrines in Berkeley Castle Service
59 Cruet frame, width 11 ins, one of a pair in Berkeley Castle Service

60 Trefoil spice box, width 4¾ ins, one of a pair in Berkeley Castle Service
61 Spice box seen from above

62 Terrine with cover, with the arms of the Duke of Orleans, by Edmé-Pierre Balzac, 1757-58

63 Terrine by Lazare Martin, Marseilles, 1758

64 Mark on the terrine

65 Terrine by Imlin, Strasbourg, c 1760
66 Mark on Strasbourg terrine

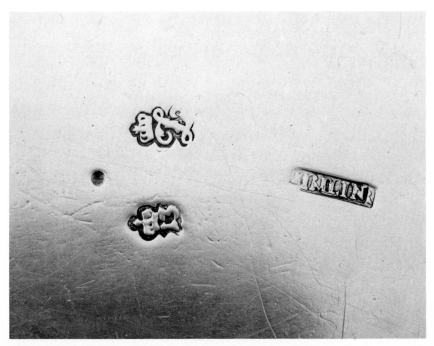

67 Terrine, maker's
mark LFD, Paris, 1787
68 Silver dish cover
from the Orloff Service
by Jacques-Nicolas
Roëttiers, Paris, 1771

69 Terrine and stand from the Orloff Service, St Petersburg mark 1784, Paris 1770-1
70 Pot-à-oille, stand and spoon by Robert-Joseph Auguste, 1784-5

71 Silver-plated Pot-à-oille, cover and stand by J. V. Huguet, c 1780

72 Terrine by Antoine Boullier, Paris, 1795-7

73 Terrine and cover from the Empress Maria Feodorovna's service by Biennais, 1809-19

76 Ewer, height 29 cm

74 Jug, height 33 cm. This and figures 73-78
are from the Empress Maria Feodorovna's
service
75 Tray, 88 cm x 51 cm

77 Stand, height 17 cm
78 Centrepiece, height 33 cm

79 Hors-d'oeuvres set by Biennais, 1810
80 Marks on hors-d'oeuvres set

gold. Madame de Pompadour's inventory, after her death in 1764, notes what is described as a *nécessaire* after designs by Falconet – a salt formed as a little fisherman seated upon a rock and holding an oyster shell, a pepper formed as a boy holding a sack, each with its little spoon; in addition there were four *couverts* of gold, a small gold spoon, two knives with jasper handles, one with a gold blade. The salt and pepper were the work of Robert-Joseph Auguste. She also owned a salt of gold formed as a basket containing a nest and two eggs on a dish of Vincennes porcelain decorated with birds, the ground *bleu celeste*, and a gold coffee pot, its heater and coffee mill. Madame du Barry, her successor as *maîtresse en chef*, employed the younger Roëttiers for a gold mustard pot, spoon and stand, and a coffee set of four cups. Queen Marie-Antoinette seems to have owned comparatively few objects in gold – merely two spoons for sugar, a small sugar tongs, a little tea-strainer, six coffee spoons, four *couverts*, two knives with gold blades, six other similar knives with pearl handles, two with ivory handles.

But all such things, even in court circles, were rarities; not so the profusion of silver and silver-gilt. For the monarch himself there were subsidiary and separate services, one for each royal residence, and also for the lesser apartments at Versailles and Fontainebleau.

Thus, in 1764, the Roëttiers, father and son, provide four dozen coffee spoons for Fontainebleau, and a tureen and a series of dishes, plates and *couverts* for use on the journeys to Compiègne and Fontainebleau. In 1749 Louis xv had offered a whole service to his daughter, the Duchess of Parma, which was made for her by F.-T. Germain. But then every member of the royal family at Versailles was entitled to his or her own service – and nearly all these magnificent pieces by the greatest craftsmen of the age disappeared during or after the Revolution. It is therefore no surprise to learn that the greatest collections of table services, as of toilet services, are to be found outside the borders of France, notably in Russia and Portugal. In addition to the Orloff service already mentioned, and not counting the various pieces sold by the Soviets between the wars, there still exists, shared between the Kremlin and the Hermitage, a vast amount of French plate which does not appear as yet to have been fully catalogued. The inventory compiled by Foelkersam in 1907 mentions four whole services supplied by Robert-Joseph Auguste to Catherine the Great ; he gives them the following names :

1. The service Ekaterinoslav (1776-8) in making which Auguste called in the help of Lenhendrick and Charles Spriman.
2. The service Kazan (1778) in which Lenhendrick again assisted.
3. The service Moscow (1782-3).
4. The service Nijégorodski (1778-9).

The earliest of the French silver which belonged to the Russian court appears to consist of three elaborate table centres attributed to Claude II Ballin. A pair of ice buckets are from the workshop of Thomas Germain while his son François-Thomas was the official silversmith to the Imperial Court. He provided the so-called Paris service (1756-9) from which the USSR sold a great tureen in 1930 (now in the Metropolitan Museum, New York) and a pair of candelabra (in the Cleveland Museum). From him also came the three table centres commissioned by the Empress Elizabeth which belonged to Prince Soltikoff (and were bought back by the Court in the nineteenth century) – Bacchus and Cupid, The Awakening of Cupid and The Infancy of Comedy.

That other silversmiths apart from the Germains and the elder Roëttiers were no less accomplished is shown by very many surviving examples, among them the imposing silver tureen (Figure 62) by Edmé-Pierre Balzac, 1757-8 (he became Master in 1739, and was still living in 1781) which he made for Philippe Egalité, Duc d'Orleans, now in the Metropolitan Museum (Wentworth Bequest) – a lovely piece of mid-eighteenth century design – celery stalks, flowing upwards and outwards from the feet to form the handles, and two savage hounds and a stricken deer for a finial. In the nineteenth century this was owned by King Louis-Philippe, who added the shield with the arms.

But more modest provincial makers, not raising their eyes to the dazzling height of a royal commission, but catering for prosperous locals, were not so far behind in quality; the tureen, for instance, of 1758 by Lazare Martin of Marseilles with its cabbage finial (Figures 63 and 64) – the same type of object was produced in delicious nuances of soft colours by the Marseilles faïence manufacturers – or the simpler, smoother, demure tureen with the pomegranate finial by Imlin of Strasbourg of about the same time (Figures 65 and 66). This is a tradition which died hard, for one finds very much the same design, only slightly more elaborate, in the tureen of 1787, by the unidentified Paris maker L. F. D. (Figure 67).

With the next three illustrations we are dealing with the work of the two greatest silversmiths of the later years of the *ancien régime*, Jacques-Nicholas Roëttiers (as distinguished a craftsman as his father, Jacques, who had been responsible for the Berkeley Service) and Robert-Joseph Auguste, who handed on the torch to his son Henry (presumably there was some English family connection, for the name is always spelt in the English fashion, not the French). The first of the Roëttiers pieces is a dish cover with a fir-cone finial in the Firestone Collection, Paris 1771 (Figure 68) and part of the great Orloff service already mentioned, which the Empress Catherine II bought back after the death of the favourite. The second, from the same service, is the majestic tureen and stand, of 1770, and with the St Petersburg mark of 1784 (Figure 69), now in the enchanting little Nissim de Camondo Museum whose garden adjoins the Parc Monceau and in which it is difficult to believe one is not back in the eighteenth century. Near it is a pair of *pots-à-oille* from the same service and of the same date and of similar design and four ice buckets and there are in the Louvre a pair of candelabra and a supper dish *en suite*. The Nissim de Camondo Museum also houses the *pot-à-oille* with its stand and spoon by Robert-Joseph Auguste, 1784, its cover surmounted by a boar's head resting on oak leaves, the acanthus foliage of the four feet spreading upwards to form the two handles (Figure 70). The spoon is formed as a large sea-shell. The coats of arms on all three pieces have not been identified; they are surmounted by a marquess' coronet, which was added later, and is thought to be English.

The second *pot-à-oille* belongs to Mr Stavros Niarchos, so good of its kind in its quiet, dignified, neo-classic manner, that it just had to be included in this volume amid silver, silver-gilt and gold, even though it is merely silver-plated; the date, about 1780, maker probably Jean-Vincent Huguet, and once in the Puiforcat Collection (Figure 71).

The small tureen with the corncob finial, also in the Niarchos Collection (Figure 72), takes us well beyond the turmoil of the Revolution itself in 1789 and the following four years, into the scarcely less agitated times of the Directory. Its date is 1795-7, its maker Antoine Boullier, the style already the formal, slightly stilted, scholarly, serious manner of the brief reign of Napoleon, which is represented to perfection by the six splendid pieces from the service which the most successful silversmith of the First Empire, Martin-Guillaume Biennais, made to the order of the Empress Maria Feodorovna (wife of Catherine II's sadistic, murdered son) between 1809 and 1819, and are now in the Rijksmuseum, Amsterdam (Figures 73-78).

A further insight into the ideals of First Empire taste is provided by the imposing hors-d'oeuvres set, with its hound finials, winged sphinx supports to the upper portion and the charming child surmounting the whole structure (Figures 79 and 80).

Another Empire-style triumph is to be seen in the sauceboat, one of a pair (Figure 81), with its easy flowing line which can be compared with the sauceboat by Charles-César Haudry of 1745 (Figure 82) in which the scroll handles rise no less felicitously from a bunch of bulrushes, with further bulrushes and foliage above. The traditional magic would appear to be no less powerful after two generations.

As an example of the finest kind of dessert service, the case of eighty pieces in its original box, silver-gilt, 1780, by Jean-Etienne Langlois (Figure 83), bearing the coat of arms of the Duc de Lorraine (Firestone Collection) can be taken as both typical and superlative.

The Bateman-Hanbury silver was dispersed at Christie's in 1926 and included the octagonal plates illustrated. Each bears the Paris date mark for 1723. One is from the Firestone Collection (Figure 84), the other is in the Louvre (Figure 85), yet others were in the Puiforcat Collection before its purchase by Mr Niarchos. They bear the arms of William Bateman, son of a Lord Mayor of London and 1st Viscount Bateman and those of his wife Lady Anne Spencer, granddaughter of the 1st Duke and Duchess of Marlborough. The marriage took place in 1720 and these octagonal plates, by Nicolas Besnier, were part of a service ordered soon afterwards, probably from Besnier, who evidently asked others to take part in what must have been an important commission, for some pieces are by Lamiche, and one by Depris. The two plates, sumptuous, severe and with a minimum of ornament, provide an engaging contrast to the flowing lines and subtle curves with moulded border of the dish of 1784 by Jean-Louis Outrebon (Figure 86).

Two years later, by Henry Auguste, comes the sauceboat and tray with its delicate engraving, the curve of the lip beautifully balanced by the handle, almost, in the current neo-classic manner of that decade, as if this really was designed as a boat with a prow and tall stern (Figure 87).

A multitude of smaller, useful tablewares from the beginning to the end of the eighteenth century have survived, among them a celebrated pair of sauceboats, now in the Musée des Arts Decoratifs, which, with the two little mustard barrels wheeled by Cupids, are the only pieces of table silver which can be definitely said to have belonged to Madame de Pompadour. The sauceboats, of which one only is illustrated (Figure 89), are by François Joubert, 1754-5, bear their owner's arms on a cartouche in the centre, and have long been recognised as superb examples of the mid-century rococo style at its distinguished best, at once playful and dignified, asymetrical in detail only, not in basic design – the handles for instance differ from one another and even the central cartouche is slightly out of balance, minute elegancies which give an immediate feeling of movement. The mustard-barrels (Figure 90), each with an eagle with outspread wings above the wheel, belong to the Gulbenkian Foundation in Lisbon, and are contained in their original leather case with the three towers of the favourite's arms. The notion is charming, the execution perfection. The arms, originally on the shields which the eagles support, have been effaced. There is another mustard-barrel of the same type in the Musée des Arts Decoratifs in which, instead of an eagle over the wheel, a hound at the side stands up on its hind legs to welcome the child. In each case the maker is Antoine-Sebastien Durand. It is just possible that, as the years pass, a few other pieces from what must have been a fabulous collection may be identified. The reign of Madame de Pompadour as principal mistress of Louis xv lasted from 1745 until her death in 1764 and during those twenty years her expenditure was phenomenal. Whatever criticisms can be levelled at her character, none can ever suggest that her taste in works of art was anything but exquisite. It is tempting to imagine her as a highly successful Minister of Fine Arts under a less corrupt régime, severely disciplined by a Soames Forsyte type of Treasury bureaucrat, and opening exhibitions here and there with more than royal grace, dressed in the grey silk in which she presides over the Jones collection in the Victoria and Albert Museum. Her heir was her brother, who by her influence had been created Marquis de Marigny and Directeur-Général des Bâtiments du Roi; within two years all had been dispersed.

Sea shells have been favourite models, and not only for silversmiths, from time immemorial (for instance, as early as about 2,000 B C in Crete), and were familiar objects for small tablewares throughout the eighteenth century in Europe – never, one may venture to say, translated into practical terms with greater finesse than in the next two illustrations, part of the Catherine D. Wentworth Bequest to the Metropolitan Museum in 1948. The first single piece, with its seaweed (?) handle is by Louis Regnard, 1753-4 (Figure 91). The second photograph is of a pair by the younger Roëttiers, Jacques-Nicolas, who retired in 1777 and is not to be confused with his no less accomplished father Jacques who retired five years earlier; these are dated 1772-3 (Figure 92). The illustration shows the bowl of one and the base of the other – superlative examples of the manner in which nature, in delicate hands, can be called upon to add to the pleasures of civilised society.

While the Pompadour's children with their wheel-barrows and barrels would obviously add to the gaiety of any supper table, the idea of a barrel for mustard was no new thing and had been in favour during the previous twenty-five years at least, as witness the two which follow, the earlier (from the Firestone Collection) by Aymé Joubert bearing the Paris date letter K for 1727 (Figure 93), the other (one of a pair from the Wentworth Bequest) is by Louis Regnard, 1740-1 (Figure 94). Two others from the same splendid bequest to the Metropolitan Museum, no less rare, provide engaging evidence of ingenuity in design. There are thirty years between them, the earlier (Figure 95), 1717-22 by Henry Adnet, clearly based upon a late seventeenth century ewer even to the curved uprising handle, the later one, 1748-9, by Guillaume Egée (Figure 96), though convincingly designated a mustard pot, is no less convincingly an adaptation, spiral fluting and all, from a much larger jug – for the style, compare a jug of 1756-7 in the Victoria and Albert Museum by Charles Donze.

Next, two small unpretentious little objects: each of them minor enchantments, once in the Puiforcat Collection. First there is the eleven-centimetre-diameter, double-handled bowl, the base curving slightly out-wards chased with acanthus leaves, the curved handles chased with foliage. Made at Morlaix about 1700 (Figure 97). The owner's name, F. Morvan is engraved on it. The other (two photographs, from side and above Figure 98) is also of provincial manufacture, by R. L. Charpentier, Rambervilliers in the Vosges – one of several wine tasters which were in the exhibition *'Le Vin de France dans l'Histoire'* at the Archives Nationales in 1953. It could scarcely be simpler or more suited to its workaday purpose. The thumb piece is formed as a fleur-de-lis pierced and engraved above a ring; here again the owner was careful to have his name engraved in large ornate capitals, J. Renant. The date – about mid eighteenth century.

The manner in which the exuberance of the more prosperous years of the reign of Louis XIV was gradually disciplined into a style remark-able for dignified simplicity – a style which, as in English silver of the same period, was puritanical by comparison with what had gone before – is seen very clearly in the circular sugar bowl and cover from the Victoria and Albert Museum of the years 1711-12 by Simon le Bastier (Figures 99 and 100) (Louis XIV died in 1715) and by the four spice boxes which follow, all of them from the next few years, and all in American collections. The earlier (Wentworth Bequest, Metropolitan Museum) (Figure 101) with its smooth oval body and paw-feet, 1719-20, is by Charles-François Croze, who became Master in the Guild in 1712 and was still living in 1754, the second (in the same bequest), 1723-4, is by Nicolas Mahon (Figure 102), while the pair with the incurved foliage feet, also 1723, by Antoine Filassier, come from the Firestone Collection (Figure 103). The sugar casters, of about 1728-9 by Nicolas Besnier (Figure 104) – intricate pierced foliage pattern above and lovely formal chasing below – were acquired by the Metropolitan in 1938, as fine a pair by one of the greatest silversmiths of the day as exists. With the two other sugar bowls, both from the Wentworth Bequest, we are half a century on and looking at, in the one instance, a late (1777-8) flower-ing of the mid-century rococo fashion (Figure 105), the maker Alex-andre de Roussy the younger, who became Master in 1758 and was still working in 1792; in the other a straightforward essay of 1786-7 in the current neoclassic manner (Figure 106), the maker Etienne Modenz – in each case nice, run-of-the-mill work by men of no particular fame.

The pair of *Verrières* (Figures 107 and 108) (the English monteith), originally in the Puiforcat Collection, are silver-gilt by the elder Auguste, Robert-Joseph, their date 1782, with lovely foliage handles; the other *Verrière* (Figure 109), one of a pair by Henry Auguste, 1789, already, particularly in the handles, looking forward to the comparative severity of post-Revolution ideals. The pair by Robert-Joseph Auguste once belonged to the Russian Court, inventory numbers 1 and 23.

Finally, going back about a hundred years, there is the pair of salad-oil bottles (Figure 110) in their stand; late seventeenth century, the stand formed as a figure of eight with three superimposed rings – objects of exceptional rarity, once in the Puiforcat Collection, to be compared for their style with the rococo cruet frame for the Berkeley Castle service (Figure 61).

Ecuelles

The *écuelle* is so characteristic a piece of French table silver that it deserves a section to itself. No doubt it had its origin in simpler days when the average person would eat from a wooden bowl and the slightly better-off from pewter. The nearest English seventeenth century equivalent is the vessel we know by the homely name of porringer, but this – much in favour in the seventeenth century – is invariably deeper than the *écuelle* in proportion to its diameter. The Scots devised a bowl much closer to the French *écuelle* – the quaich. This though was rarely if ever provided with a cover, and always had two lugs projecting at right angles from the upper part of the bowl. The *écuelle* generally had this feature, but not always, as witness the two illustrated here – the one of 1670 (Figure 111), the other of about 1800. Each of them have handles. Though one does occasionally come across an English porringer and cover which could, by a little exercise of the imagination, be described as at least a first cousin of an *écuelle*, this particular type of vessel did not, for reasons difficult to explain, become fashionable with us in spite of its obvious usefulness and the possibilities provided by its essentially elegant proportions for a gifted designer. That these possibilities are infinite is shown to great advantage in these nine examples.

The first, from the Firestone Collection, is the earliest, Paris 1670 and by an unknown maker – snake handle on the cover resting on a cut cord pattern, scroll handles – a more than ordinary rarity. The second, by Sebastien Leblond, 1690-2, is unique (Figure 112), the only example of royal plate which has come down to us. It was made for Le Grand Dauphin, son of Louis XIV and heir to the throne, and consequently of exceptional interest. It bears the Dauphin's arms, and the cover has a hinged handle above a splendidly chased design of foliage. The two ears at each side are cast and chased with dolphins and shells. It was not, it seems, the custom at this period to make a stand or plate upon which to rest an *écuelle* – the case in which this one is fitted has no place for any addition; stands do not appear until about 1730. Nor were the contents eaten with a spoon; the vessel was picked up by its two ears and brought to the lips.

81 Sauceboat on stand by Claude Mennessier, overall height 10 ins, Paris, 1819-38
82 Sauceboat, one of a pair by Charles-César Haudry, length 225 mm, 1745

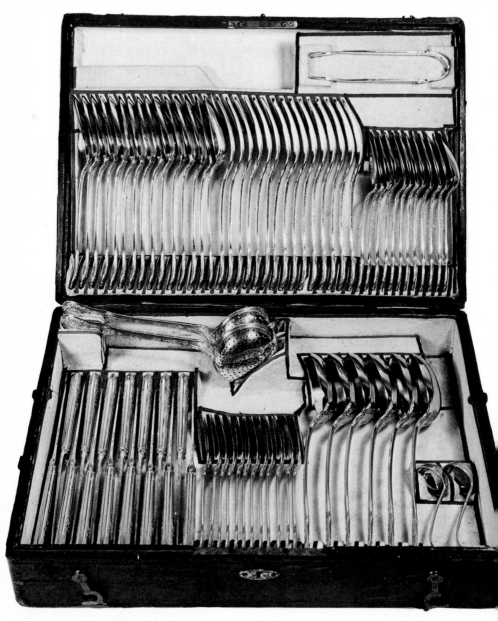

83 Silver-gilt dessert service, originally comprising 80 pieces, by Jean-Etienne Langlois, 1780

84 and 85 A pair of octagonal plates
from the Bateman service by
Nicolas Besnier

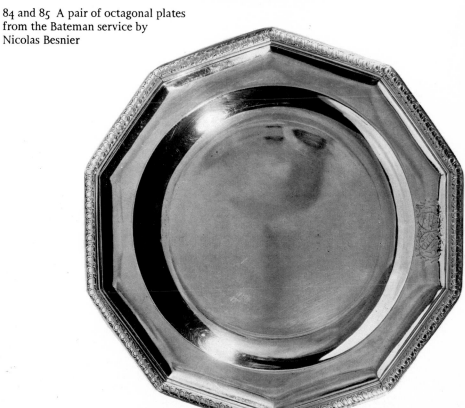

86 Dish, length 19¼ ins, by Jean-Louis Outrebon, 1784

87 Sauceboat and stand by Henry Auguste, 1786

89 Sauceboat with arms of Madame de Pompadour, 12½ cm, by François Joubert, 1754-55

90 Pair of mustard barrels, height 18 cm, by Antoine-Sébastien Durand, 1750-51

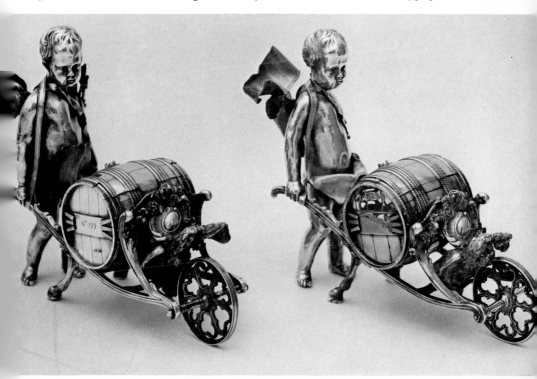

91 Shell-shaped dish by Louis Regnard, 1753-4

92 Pair of shell-shaped dishes by Jacques-Nicolas Roëttiers, 1772-73

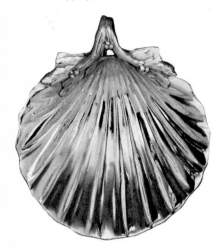

93 Mustard barrel, height 3½ ins, by Aymé Joubert, 1727

94 Mustard pot, 3⅝ ins, one of a pair by Louis Regnard, 1740-1

95 Mustard pot, height 5 ⁷⁄₁₆ ins, by Henry Adnet, 1717-22

96 Mustard pot by Guillaume Egée, 1748-9

97 Two-handled bowl, diameter 11 cm, Morlaix, c 1700

98A Wine taster by R. L. Charpentier, Rambervilliers, c 1750

98B Wine taster seen from above

99 Sugar bowl, height 5⅝ ins, by
Simon le Bastier, 1711-12
100 Marks on sugar bowl

101 Spice box with grater, height 2¼ ins, by by Charles-François Croze, 1719-20

102 Spice box, height 2½ ins, by Nicolas Mahon 1723-4

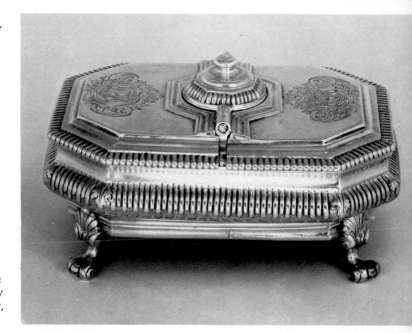

103 Pair of spice boxes, 2⅝ ins, by Antoine Filassier, 1723

104 Pair of sugar casters by Nicolas Besnier, 1728-9
105 Sugar bowl, height 5⅜ ins, with cover and tray, height ¾ in, by Alexandre de Roussy the younger, 1777-8

107 Pair of *Verrières* (monteiths) by Robert-Joseph
Auguste, 1782
108 Mark on monteiths

106 Sugar bowl with cover by Etienne Modenz,
1786-87

109 *Verrière*, height 5¼ ins, one of a pair by Henry Auguste, 1789
110 Pair of salad-oil bottles, late 17th century

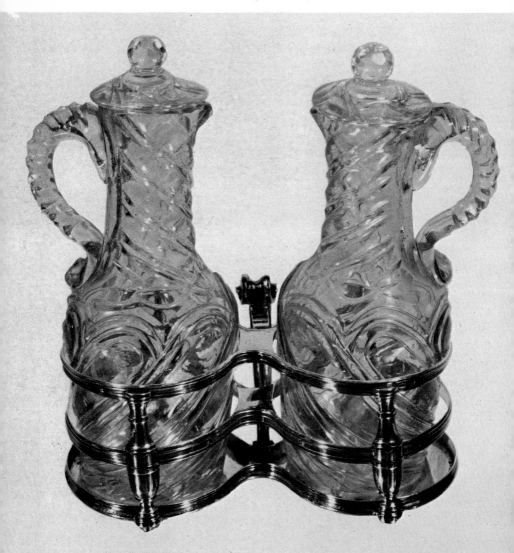

A less elaborate *écuelle* follows (Figure 113), thought to be by one of the Fauveau family of Troyes, presumably a few years later – say during the first twenty years of the eighteenth century – and a superlative example of provincial workmanship.

The dignified *écuelle* after this, each ear and the cover finial decorated with a profile head, the cover chased with a formal foliage design, bears the maker's mark of Pierre Jarrin and the date letter for 1714 (Figures 114 and 115); later in the century it found its way to Spain, of which the Madrid mark of 1782 is convincing evidence. By now the cover is beginning to rise, and most of the *écuelles* made during the following half-century have these swelling, dome-shaped covers. But not all, for of the two highly original *écuelles* of Figures 116 and 117, only one has any very marked curvature ; each is a little masterpiece in its own manner, each is highly original, and each – which one could hardly guess by merely judging from their respective styles – is by the same man in the same year, no less a person than Thomas Germain. The year is 1733-4 and no two objects could better emphasise the range and quality of this great silversmith's imagination than these *écuelles*, for in the first, with its snake handles both at each side and on the cover and in the extreme simplicity of its line, he has gone back to the world of 1670 which produced the sober elegance of the first *écuelle* illustrated, whereas in the other he shows himself in complete command of the idiom – the rococo idiom – which was by this time *à la mode*. This is marvellously subtle design, at once playful and majestic ; and it is no wonder that it is regarded with something like awe. It was made for the Portuguese Cardinal de Motta and is one of the few pieces in existence which can bring to mind something of the quality of the plate Thomas Germain supplied to the House of Braganza during his working life and which perished in the Lisbon earthquake of 1755. A tray *en suite* was made for this and is also at the Louvre.

The domed cover and the artichoke, or similar vegetable finial, remained popular for less august pieces for many years, as witness the fine *écuelle*, cover and stand, with its celery leaves and artichoke finial by Michel de Lapierre, Paris, 1750, belonging to the Niarchos Collection (Figure 118), and the one of about 1760 by Pierre-Guillaume Rahier of Brest (Figure 119) (it is undated but Rahier became Master in 1744). Finally, there is the demure little *écuelle* and stand of about 1800 with its delicate engraving and rectangular handles (Figure 120). We are back – more or less – to the comparative simplicity, if not the generous majestic volumes, of 1670.

Chocolate, Tea and Coffee

The homely vessel, the chocolate pot of Figure 121, from the Firestone Collection, made in the first years of the eighteenth century, is a useful reminder that not all such things were devised by great men for the great, and that there must have been an immense quantity of similar Plain Jane pots of various sorts in circulation among ordinary people. This, a considerable rarity, provides a notable contrast to the sophistication of all except one of the remaining objects in this section.

The teapot (Figures 122 and 123) with its grooved form and festoons of applied floral, foliage decoration, silver-gilt, is by some unknown Paris maker of 1732-3. The next, a plain teapot of 1750 by Nicolas Outrebon (Firestone Collection) (Figure 124) has all the quiet dignity one associates with a painting of pots by Chardin put together with far more skill than the first illustration with its endearing kitchen clumsiness, as indeed one would expect from a silversmith of such accomplishment as Outrebon – no pretty tricks, but a beautiful smooth shape and a handle and thumb-piece worthy of a tankard. Again, one cannot fail to notice how, in the midst of all kinds of rococo whimsies, solid, sensible, comely, practical vessels were still being turned out.

The jug by Charles Donze (Figures 125 and 126), with its easy spirals, is a delightful example of a fashion which had a long run, for a similar design is to be seen in the little mustard pot of 1748 in the Metropolitan Museum (Figure 96), in the *verseuse* (jug for hot water or milk) of 1772 by Duguay (Figure 128) (Niarchos Collection) and in many other examples outside the borders of France, particularly in Germany and Holland; the pattern was clearly popular over a wide area.

But of all French vessels of this character from the great period of the craft, the most distinguished are surely the two in silver-gilt in the Niarchos Collection which follow, their maker Louis-Joseph Lenhendrick (Figures 127 and 129). The small one, still kept in its original red leather case, is dated 1774, the larger 1770. For sheer quality of engraving, chasing, and elegant form they are incomparable.

With the little silver-gilt milk jug of 1778 by A.-N. Cousinet (Figure

130) we are almost back to the simplicity of the early part of the century.

Finally a silver-gilt *nécessaire* or travelling tea-and-coffee service, by Biennais (Figure 131), each piece engraved with the arms or monogram of Napoleon I and of the Archduchess Marie-Louise of Austria whom he married in 1810. The service is contained in a brass inlaid mahogany case with the same armorials in the centre of the lid and a secret compartment with a pin hole operating the concealed catch. It was a gift from the Emperor to his wife and, at her death in 1847, became the property of her great-nephew, the Archduke Louis-Victor of Habsburg. It remains a notable example of First Empire taste.

Two Frames

Among the silver furniture which was so greatly admired and envied at Versailles when the Sun King was at his most splendid must have been this silver-gilt frame, its date Paris 1672, which came to the Victoria and Albert Museum with the Jones Bequest (Figure 132 and 133). It has no maker's mark, but is attributed to the hand of Nicolas Delaunay, one of the several masters who contributed to the extravagant embellishment of the palace, and particularly of the Galerie des Glaces, during the early years of the reign. Today the very notion of furniture made from silver seems distasteful, the king's ambitions little more than swollen-headed dreams. But while the dreams lasted, king, courtiers and foreigners believed in them. Next to nothing is left of all these seventeenth century marvels and we have to depend upon the evidence of a few tapestries designed by Charles Lebrun who placed in them many of the great silver pieces he had himself caused to be fashioned, and the careful lists compiled for the *Compte des bâtiments du Roi sous le règne de Louis* XIV, *L'inventaire général du mobilier de la Couronne sous Louis* XIV (both published by Jules Guiffrey) and the *Journal du Garde-Meuble*. Beginning at the latest in 1666, and probably earlier, in 1661, a prodigious amount of silver furniture, silver vases, torchères and other objects, in addition to scarcely less extravagant pieces for sideboard, dining and dressing table, all from Le Brun's design, were commissioned from the finest silversmith of the day. The last pieces were executed in 1686. Three years later most went to the melting pot, and twenty years after that the little which remained was melted down. Very few of these major works escaped. One of them is a great double-handled fountain 64 centimetres in height, of the year 1661, in the Lopez-Willshaw Collection, which, though slightly less ornate, is very close to a fountain in the series of Gobelins tapestries by Le Brun entitled *L'Histoire du Roi*. It bears an unidentified English coat of arms and was no doubt sent to England soon after it was made in the reign of Charles II. The other, more famous piece, which was not made for the French court, nor in Paris, but which gives a very good idea of the grandiose style of these years is the baptismal font made for the King of Sweden between 1696 and 1707 by

Jean-François Cousinet who, trained by his father in Paris, settled in Stockholm in 1693.

The Victoria and Albert Museum frame was no doubt made to contain either a royal portrait or a scene of some military triumph; above Fame sounds her trumpet with the boastful inscription '*Fama ingens ingentior armis*' which can be rather clumsily interpreted as 'Great Fame grows yet greater by Arms'. The symbolism of the base is clear enough and no less boastful, for the gallic cock holds in leash with its beak the imperial eagle of Austria on one side and the two lions of Holland and Spain on the other. With the frame and the medallion contained in it of Figure 134 we are in a more gracious, less pompous age: a silver frame by Pierre Germain (le Roman) enclosing a delicate gold low-relief river landscape with a fisherman by the sculptor Michel Clodion, the date 1776.

Although the Victoria and Albert frame is ascribed to Charles Delaunay on the grounds of style, in the splendid volume *Les Grands Orfèvres de Louis* XIII *à Charles* X (to which this more modest production is so greatly indebted), it is suggested that it could very well have been made by Pierre Germain. 'Style' in any decade can easily mean that artists express themselves in a common language, and this frame, failing definite proof, could have come from the workshop of any one of a dozen competent silversmiths. On page 51 of the chapter devoted to the Germain family is a reference to the *Mercure de France* of November 1677, quoted from Bapst. In that reference the description exactly fits this frame. The puzzling feature is the date, but the quotation definitely refers to Pierre Germain, father of the famous Thomas Germain, as the maker. Unless Bapst made an error in the date of the issue of the *Mercure de France* from which he quotes, it seems impossible to discount this evidence, viz that Germain did actually make a frame decorated in this grandiose manner to contain a portrait of the King by Benard which was presented by the Abbé le Houx. If Delaunay or someone else made such a frame in 1672 it might have been used for another portrait on another and earlier occasion and Pierre Germain might have been commissioned to make a replica four or five years later – or, and this seems more likely, he might have made the frame in 1672-3 in accordance with measurements given by the painter, who proceeded to fill the frame at leisure – and then at last the Reverend Abbé made his presentation. The point is of no great importance. The frame remains a superb example of baroque pomposity, extravagant sycophancy and consummate craftsmanship.

Candlesticks and Candelabra

One magnificent pair of candelabra by Thomas Germain is referred to in the later section on the Germain family and is illustrated in Figure 164; and another, a three-branch candelabra, is by Duvivier made from a design by Meissonnier. It seems appropriate to provide a brief survey here of the styles in vogue during rather more than a century from 1675 until the Revolution of 1789.

The pair of cluster column candlesticks by Pierre Masse, 1675 (Figure 135), with their intricate chasing, are typical of the luxurious fashions of the heyday of Louis XIV and there is no need for any Englishman to look further to discover where silversmiths working in London during the reigns of Charles II and James II obtained their ideas. Not everything, even in so luxurious an age, was quite so elaborate, and the pair by Charles Delafond (Figure 136), five and a half inches high as compared with the seven inches of the former, are as demure as anyone could wish – date 1680, and, judging by their size, from some dispersed toilet-table set. Both pairs are from the Firestone Collection.

The dignified candlestick next, its high-shouldered stem set with a profile head, is one of a set of four of the year 1719 (the marks on the base exceptionally clear), by Gilles Govel (Figures 137 and 138). This was a style destined to last for many years in spite of the undeniable influence of Meissonnier's designs, for the candlestick of Figure 139, from the Firestone Collection, one of a set of four, belongs to the year 1740, by Edmé-Pierre Balzac, three years later than the pair of two-branch candelabra (Figure 140) – or rather, three years later than their stems, which are more elaborately chased than the Balzac candlesticks. They also are from the Firestone silver, the stems by François Riel, 1737, the branches – beautifully flowing foliage shapes – 1739 by Jacques Duguay. Neither in France nor elsewhere was it uncommon for the branches to be added to a single candlestick by a different silver-smith.

The next pair (Figure 141) – still the high-shouldered stem (glass collectors will see in it some resemblance to the so called Silesian stem) – is by Louis Regnard, 1743, belonging to Mr Niarchos : a well-known

46

and magnificent pair, once in the Puiforcat Collection, recorded as far back as 1880 in the San Donato sale, and exhibited in a Paris exhibition in 1926, in London in 1933 in the exhibition 'Three French Reigns', and, in 1938, in the exhibition 'French Domestic Silver' at the Metropolitan Museum, New York, to the catalogue of which, by Faith Dennis, every student of the subject is so greatly indebted.

The remaining two are from the Catherine D. Wentworth Bequest to the Metropolitan Museum in 1948. The first, with four branches, is one of a pair, the date 1768-9, maker Jean-Baptiste-François Chéret (Figure 142) ; the style is sobering down a little, but the foliage details are still asymmetrically gay, whereas in the no less distinguished pair which follows the neo-classics have won a resounding victory – everything neat and formal and, as far as anyone knew, à la Grecque. We have very nearly reached the rather stiff mannerisms – all dignity but not much fluidity, of the style which was to dominate the whole field of the applied arts until after Waterloo. The maker in this instance is Henry Auguste, the date 1788-9, that is, the eve of the Revolution (Figure 143).

Miscellaneous

Finally, four pieces which do not come into any of the previous categories. There is first a most unusual object from the Firestone Collection – a small marble tobacco box with silver mounts, 1756-7, by François Joubert (Figure 144). Next comes an oval basin from the Wentworth Bequest at the Metropolitan Museum, which presumably began life as a dish for the table, 1745-6, its maker Jean Fauche who was born before 1706 and became Master in 1733 and died in 1762. In 1760-1 Duguay added the chin piece and so turned it into a shaving dish (Figure 145).

This book does not deal with ecclesiastical silver, which requires separate treatment. It has been, however, difficult to resist this silver-gilt chalice and paten from the Victoria and Albert Museum, mid-seventeenth century (Figure 146). The maker's mark on the chalice, B.P. beneath a fleur-de-lis. It came from the Convent of the Visitation, Rouen, a fine example of the rich decoration which was the mark of those years, flowers and foliage and winged cherubs – the winged cherubs which became such favourite ornaments on English and other clocks during the last half of the century.

Ecuelles

111 *Ecuelle*, Paris, 1670
112 *Ecuelle*, by Sébastien Leblond, 1690-92

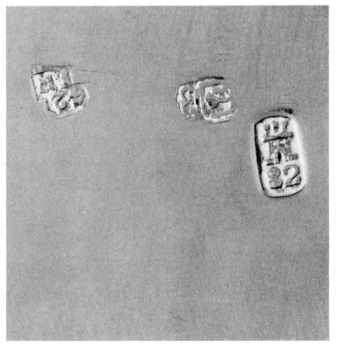

113 Silver-gilt *Ecuelle* and cover by Pierre Jarrin, 1714
114 Marks on the *Ecuelle* including the Madrid mark of 1782

115 *Ecuelle*, length 10⅞ ins, by one of the Fauveau family of Troyes, early 18th century
116 *Ecuelle* by Thomas Germain, 1733-34

117 Silver-gilt *Ecuelle* by Thomas Germain, 1733-34
118 *Ecuelle* and stand by Michel de Lapierre, Paris, 1750, stand 1745

119 *Ecuelle* by Pierre-Guillaume Rahier, Brest, c 1760
120 *Ecuelle* with cover and dish, diameter 7½ ins, by Marc Jacquait, c 1800

Chocolate, Tea and Coffee

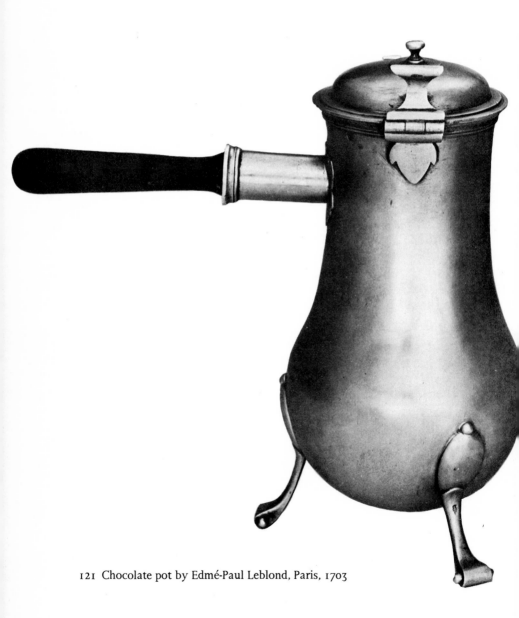

121 Chocolate pot by Edmé-Paul Leblond, Paris, 1703

122 Silver-gilt teapot, height 5⅝ ins, Paris, 1732-3
123 Paris mark on teapot

124 Teapot by Nicolas Outrebon, Paris, 1750

125 Jug, height 7⅜ ins, by Charles Donze. Paris, 1756-8
126 Mark on jug

127 Two silver-gilt coffee pots by Louis-
Joseph Lenhendrick, 1770 and 1774

128 Jug by Joseph-Pierre-Jacques Duguay,
1772
129 Mark on smaller coffee pot figure 128

130 Silver-gilt milk jug by Ambroise-Nicolas Cousinet, 1778

131 Silver-gilt tea and coffee service by Martin-Guillaume Biennais

Two Frames

132 Silver-gilt frame, height 12⅛ ins, attributed to Nicolas Delaunay, possibly by Pierre Germain, Paris, 1672

133 Detail from the silver-gilt frame

133A One of a pair of spoons by T. Germain, Paris, 1735. Length 11⅞ ins. A recent discovery (1969) in London

134 Silver frame by Pierre Germain 'le Roman', enclosing a gold river landscape by Clodion, 1776

Designs for Silver

Strapwork, masks and formal patterns provide the age of Louis XIV with a great deal of its dignity and not a little of its pomposity; to this the designs for silver by Le Sieur Masson, the frontispiece to whose pattern book is illustrated here (Figure 147), bear eloquent witness. The seventeenth century had been rich in Admirable Crichtons of the calibre of Le Brun, who imposed his will upon every department of the arts. At least one man of a later generation could and did claim a similar eminence, Juste-Aurèle Meissonier – painter, sculptor, architect, etc.: 'Dessinateur de la Chambre et Cabinet du Roy'. The title page of his *Oeuvre*, first part (Figures 148 and 149), leaves us in no doubt that he had a good opinion of himself and is, in itself, an epitome of the style which he did as much as anyone to introduce – a style all sweetness and light and asymmetrical which, for want of a better word, we label Rococo. He was able and willing to turn his hand to anything. He would design you a home, and its contents from cellar to attic. Nothing was too great or too small – scissors, knobs for sticks, watch cases, gold sword guards for the wedding of Louis XV in 1725, tables, a small sledge for the Dowager Queen of Spain in 1735, a painted ceiling for the church of St Sulpice. It is a little puzzling that such a man could also be classed as a Master Silversmith, and it is more than probable that the Guild never regarded him as a genuine member of their community. The Paris silversmiths however had to accept him because he was made Master in 1724 'par Brevet du Roi', a rare, and much valued favour. The king in that year was fourteen years of age and would have given Meissonier the Brevet at the request of the Duc de Bourbon for whom he had made some table silver the previous year.

Of the designs from his extremely fertile brain which were actually carried out we reproduce the *seau à refraîcheur* (Figure 150) which was executed for Monseigneur le Duc in 1723 – the Duc's arms in the centre, merman and mermaid at each side, Neptune in relief below, and a Monstrance made in 1727 for a house of Carmelite Nuns at Poitiers (Figure 151). But by 1735 his inventiveness reached the height of playful extravagance in his designs for a great table centrepiece and

49

two tureens (Figure 152) which were made that year for the Duke of Kingston, an enchanting riot of fish, game, Cupids, cabbages and various vegetables which would no doubt be accounted one of the wonders of the world had they survived. (Rumour, by the way, asserts that the tureens are actually in existence; buried in some bank vault – a rumour which will be disbelieved until they emerge.) Their original owner was the personage whom Horace Walpole described as 'a very weak man, of the greatest beauty and finest person in England'. He was Evelyn Pierre-pont, 2nd Duke of Kingston (1711-73) who succeeded his grandfather in 1726. An even shrewder observer than Walpole, his aunt, Lady Mary Wortley Montagu, had this comment to make: 'The Duke of Kingston has hitherto had so ill an education, 'tis hard to make any judgment of him; he has his spirit but I fear will never have his father's sense, as young noblemen go, 'tis possible he may make a good figure among them.' He did in fact carry out the obligations of that station in life to which Providence had called him, holding various public offices, raising a Regiment of Light Horse during the '45, and receiving the K.G., but he is best remembered for his long association with Elizabeth Chudleigh, wife of Augustus John Hervey, later 3rd Earl of Bristol; she became his mistress in 1760, and her story is said to have suggested to Thackeray the character of Beatrice in *Henry Esmond* and of the Baroness Bernstein in *The Virginians*.

Meissonnier, as silversmith, used as his mark the initials J.O.M. and a fleur-de-lis crowned. (The O was evidently considered a reasonable compromise for the Aur of Aurelius.) Among the other Meissonnier designs is one described simply as *Nef pour le Roy* (Figure 153), and an elaborate candelabra, also for the King, described as a project, which presumably was never actually executed (Figure 154).

The two tureens, the one surmounted by fish (Figure 155), the other with a simple vegetable finial (Figure 156), are characterisic examples of his self-confident ingenuity from this pattern book, while the mounts for the pair of salad-oil bottles (Figure 157) (very similar to several which actually exist) provide yet further evidence of his ability to devise comely objects which are at once practical and playful. The design for the candlestick is one more instance of the grace and fluidity of the style which he did so much to impose upon a whole generation; he seems to have been particuarly proud of them, for he is careful to emphasise that they were his invention in 1728 (Figures 158 and 159).

Finally there is his design for the stem of a candlestick (Figure 160) to be compared with its translation into metal in the splendid three-branch candelabra by Claude Duvivier, 1734-5, in the Musée des Arts Decoratifs (Figures 161 and 162).

The Rise and Fall of the House of Germain

As a general rule notable practitioners in the applied arts rarely leave much behind them beyond their reputation and their works. Sometimes it is their reputation alone which has survived, all the fine things upon which that reputation was built having perished. Nor have we any notion of what kind of men they were, whether tall or short, dark or fair, or know whether they had other interests apart from their work, who were their friends, how they lived and died. No Boswell followed them about, noting their conversation, no dispenser of social gossip dined out on their epigrams, very few painters took the trouble to do their portraits.

In this respect the first of the three distinguished Paris silversmiths, Pierre, Thomas and François-Thomas Germain – grandfather, son and grandson – was particularly unfortunate, for, as far as is known, all his work for the Crown perished in the two desperate attempts made by Louis XIV to restore the kingdom's shaky finances. In the first of these, in 1689, it was only the more elaborate and ornamental items of gold and silver which were sent to the melting pot, but the table services followed eleven years after; consequently one is left to guess at the extent and quality of the silver commissioned from Pierre Germain by the court by reference to official inventories and from the evidence provided by Gobelins tapestries which often show silver as part of Versailles.

Pierre Germain was the son of a silversmith, François, and was born in Paris in 1645. He was admitted Master in the Guild in 1669, as his father's pupil. He is first heard of at the age of seventeen when Colbert, the King's chief minister and as dedicated an administrator as ever existed, advised almost certainly by Charles le Brun, presented him to Louis XIV. He was commissioned to make bindings for the books which recorded the victories of the reign, and carried out the work in gold, depicting Louis with his left hand resting on a shield and slaves prostrating themselves before him. In 1677, he made a frame for a portrait of the king by Benard, which was presented to the monarch by the Abbé Le Houx. A description of this frame appeared in the *Mercure de France* in November of that year. No flattery was too great for the seventeenth century royalty and the account in the *Mercure* makes strange reading today. 'At the top of the frame is Fame in relief. With one hand she points to the King, in the other she holds a trumpet. . . . A Latin inscription informs us that if this august Monarch is great on account of the glory which his fine qualities have gained for him, he is even greater because of his courage and his conquests. At the sides of the border are two children holding flowers and fruit. Nothing can be better designed. Beneath one sees the Triple Alliance in submission to France, represented by a cock. On one side the cock holds the eagle of the Empire in chains, on the other two lions flee from the cock. One lion represents Spain, the other (*un lyon marin* [sic]) Holland.'* In 1679 Germain was granted lodgings in the Louvre, and in the following year he made a cross and six silver chandeliers, engraved with the Royal Arms, for the chapel at Fontainebleau and then, in 1683, a great silver bowl, also engraved with the Royal Arms, which appears in a tapestry and which it is thought was used at the ceremonial levée. Later that year he delivered to the Garde-Meuble de la Couronne two six-branch chandeliers, and another of eight branches, evidently more elaborate, for Versailles. His fellow silversmiths Cousinet, Merlin and de Launay each provided a similar chandelier. In addition to his work for Louis XIV, Germain also supplied silver for the Dauphin whose apartment in the palace was regarded as the finest and most luxurious at Versailles, notably a silver balustrade surmounted by two vases, and – on 19 August 1684 – a great chandelier with movable silver branches attached to eight human heads, also of silver. Some idea of the splendour and luxury of the Dauphin's rooms can be obtained from contemporary documents – e.g. *Comptes des bâtiments du Roi*, 1685, mentions a massive silver table by Ballin, supported by four children seated on dolphins at a cost of 62,259 livres. Félibien in his *Description du château de Versailles* becomes a trifle breathless: 'It is in the apartment of Monseigneur that one sees an exquisite collection of everything which is most rare and precious, not only the necessary furniture – tables, cabinets, porcelain, lustres and girandoles – but paintings by the most excellent masters, bronzes, agate vases, all kinds of objects of precious metals and the finest oriental stones. The third of these rooms, which has a door leading on to the lower gallery in the centre of the château, has on all sides and in the ceiling mirrors set in gilded borders on a base of ebony marquetry. The floor is also made of choice wood embellished with many ornaments, among them the cyphers of Monseigneur and Madame la Dauphine.'

* It is suggested that the frame in the Victoria and Albert Museum (Jones Bequest) may possibly be the one referred to. (See Figures 132 and 133).

Within a few years the silver was in the melting pot. I quote Dangeau for 3 December 1689: 'The King wishes that throughout the kingdom everyone shall take to the Mint all silversmiths' works in the rooms, such as mirrors, firedogs, girandoles and every kind of vases; and, to set an example, he is melting down all his fine silver without regard to the beauty of its workmanship. He is even melting down filigree. The toilet sets of all the Ladies-in-Waiting will also be melted down, not excepting that of Madame la Dauphine.' By this drastic sacrifice the King hoped to acquire six million livres – in fact, the total came to about three million. The original cost is estimated at not less than five times that amount. Thus perished the work for the Crown, fashioned most of it in 1684 and 1685 by Pierre Germain, by Cousinet, by Ballin, and by several others. One piece alone of these royal seventeenth-century commissions has survived – a silver-gilt *écuelle*, now in the Louvre, made for le Grand Dauphin, eldest son of Louis XIV, in 1692, by Sebastien Leblond (Figure 112).

Pierre died in 1684, aged 39, at the height of his powers, leaving seven children, a great reputation and very little money. His principal room, according to the inventory made after his death, contained seven paintings valued at 27 livres, six chairs, an armchair and ten stools – total 47 livres. His workroom contained an old Bergamo tapestry valued at 10 livres. The linen included twelve pairs of sheets. His widow, Marguerite Décour, daughter of a prosperous hatter, remained in the apartment at the Louvre for three months supervising the execution of outstanding orders and collecting the sums due to her late husband. On 19 August 1685 she handed over three large silver *guéridons*, their supports formed as three female figures. In 1680 Pierre Germain had taken as apprentice François Vincent, who married Pierre's sister Françoise, and the inventory of the contents of the workshop notes that these two were witness to the fact that the widow had to sell some furniture and household utensils in order to buy what was necessary to complete the work in hand. Nothing is known about the later years of Marguerite Germain, beyond the fact that she lived to be eighty-seven and returned to live in the Louvre in the apartment of her son, Thomas.

Thomas Germain (1673-1748)

When his father died, Thomas was eleven, the eldest of seven children. While Pierre Germain had left behind him little beyond a first class reputation, the family, thanks to Madame Germain's father, was in no real difficulty. All seven went to live with their grandfather, and their uncle by marriage, François Vincent, gave Thomas his first lessons in design. Later he sent the boy to the painter Boulogne for further training. In 1686 the Academy awarded him a medal and in 1688, under the patronage of Louvois, he was sent to Rome. When his sponsor Louvois died in 1691 he became apprenticed to an Italian silversmith, with permission to go daily to the Vatican for further study. He was obviously a young man of more than ordinary accomplishments for within a very short time he was employed by the Jesuits in the construction of the nine foot high silver statue of St Ignatius for the altar of their new church (a statue destined to be destroyed by Germain's compatriots in the 1790s), and also in chiselling the bas-reliefs; statue and altar had been designed by Pierre Legros, the Protestant sculptor, whose father had fled from France after the promulgation of the Edict of Nantes in 1685. This commission led to others, including one from the Grand-Duke of Tuscany, Cosimo III, for various medallions and trophies and for two great basins which, according to the *Mercure de France*, were decorated with bas-reliefs illustrating the history of the Medicis. On his way home in 1701, he stopped at Leghorn and there designed and, it seems, supervised the building of a church – a reminder that he was something more than a brilliant silversmith. He designed yet another church nearly forty years later after the collapse in 1739 of the church of St Thomas du Louvres, when seven canons perished. Cardinal de Fleury gave him this commission and the construction of the new building, dedicated to St Louis, began in 1740. J. F. Blondel, in his *Architecture française*, 1754, has high praise for this design. By 1706 he was home, already enjoying a considerable reputation, but thanks to the financial troubles of the final years of the reign of Louis XIV, unable to find immediate scope for his exceptional gifts. Until the 1720s he seems to have made nothing for the Court and most of his work was performed for churches. He made a silver censer for the chapel at Fontainebleau which, when it was shown to the king, caused the latter to remark that 'he still remembered with pleasure the merit of his father'. In 1708 he played a part in the decoration of Notre-Dame, executing trophies for one of the pillars of the choir, and, in 1716, the Chapter commissioned him to make a silver-gilt monstrance to take the place of one by Ballin which was too heavy to carry in procession. The inventory of 1723 of the Treasury of Notre-Dame describes this piece as follows: 'Ears of wheat and grapes form the branch [presumably the stem], the glory whence the rays issue is decorated all around with clouds and heads of cherubim before and behind, the centre circle is of the same size as that in the great sun being the same crystal, the same gold cross – the same sun as the great one, which can serve for the small one. The said sun, weighing with its glory, its stem and its foot, together, thirty-two marcs.' As a result of this monstrance Thomas Germain was called in again, this time to make a cross and six great chandeliers in bronze, for the principal altar – apparently the only work in bronze he was called upon to execute. The chandeliers were required for special occasions, when they shared the altar with six of silver. Germain contracted to complete the work within a year and the price was fixed at 4,000 livres, not counting the value of the copper which was provided by Notre-Dame; the artist was responsible for the cost of the designs and the models. The design was first vetted by De Launay, a distinguished silversmith and, at that time, what we should call Master of the Mint, acting for the Chapter and, on behalf of Germain, by Coysevox, director of the Royal Academy of painting and sculpture. It is interesting that up to 1720, in spite of what on paper were stringent regulations, Germain was able to practise his craft without becoming Master in the Guild. In January of that year, however, his name appears in the register for the first time, with his brother-in-law Leonard Lagneau as guarantor – his mark T.G. and a fleece. He was now an official member of the Corporation, whereas previously he had been able to exercise his profession only as 'King's silversmith and sculptor'. In the same year he married Denise Gauchelet, daughter of a silversmith of the rue du Roule, François Gauchelet, who had been admitted Master in 1692 and had died in 1715. His next important commission was in 1722 when he made a silver-gilt sun for the coronation of Louis xv at Rheims (where all French monarchs were crowned) and which the King presented to the Cathedral. The *Mercure de France* describes it in detail in November:

Apart from the spendour lent by the precious stones which adorn it, it is impossible to set a value upon this piece. On it are two angels; one of them, St. Michael, protector of France and of the Order which bears his name, offers God the royal sword, the other presents the crown. In the middle is a cartouche with the arms of France. On the other side is this inscription: 'Louis xv, King of France, crowned at Rheims in the eighth year of his reign, the 25th October 1722, by Armand Jules de Rohan, archbishop, Duke of this Town, Premier Peer of France, made on the day of his consecration this gift to the Church of Rheims.'

The arch of the Alliance is represented in low relief on the front face of the foot, the attributes of the Evangelists are at the four angles. On the foot rises a column of clouds, representing the cloud which preceded God's people. One sees there also the symbols of the two kinds of the Eucharist— ears of corn and grapes. The Holy Spirit, the soul of saintly actions, presides at the top of this cloud which seems to dissolve to form a glory of angels and cherubim around the sun, all brilliant with rays.

One can only give the slightest idea of the execution of this work. The figures are alive and in learned taste, the draperies clinging [this seems the best translation of *sveltes* in this context] and light, the clouds well cast and seemingly vaporous and transparent, the rays luminous, the ornaments managed with wisdom, the castings with art. Everything is beautifully proportioned. One could say after examining each part in detail, that matter has changed its nature and that painting, in complete accord with sculpture, has lent the latter the effect of its light and its tones. In the opinion of connoisseurs the last degree of perfection in this kind of work resides in just this, which we owe to the invention of Bernini.

Not everyone was over-pleased at the suggestion that Thomas Germain was subject to Italian influence and the *Journal de Verdun* in December 1723 stated that this sun in the Cathedral of Rheims was merely based on the sun belonging to Notre-Dame. The *Mercure* would have none of this and in January 1723 thundered a reply:

The excellent workman who has executed this beautiful piece [*beau morceau*] after his own models, far from copying anyone, has the reputation of never repeating himself. One is well aware of the fecund genius of Germain, who treats silverwork as would a clever sculptor and whose father, employed with distinction under the reign of Louis the Great, finds himself worthily replaced by the son; he has spent a part of his life at Rome in studying the lovely remains of antiquity and has left there various monuments of his own.

This sun is also described in the *Almanach de Rheims* of 1776:

This Sun, the work of famous Germain, is not finished; if the artist had been able to give final touches, one could point to this monstrance as one of the most beautiful existing in France.

The inventory of the Cathedral in 1790 has this brief entry 'The sun of Louis xv in silver-gilt, work of Germain'. We shall never be able to form our own judgment. It is not mentioned in the inventory of 1792. The Constituent Assembly had in the meantime laid down that churches could keep only the most simple and least precious objects – those which were indispensable. It is therefore almost certain that in 1791 the sun was consigned to the melting pot.

In August 1723 Germain was granted lodgings in the Louvre and a month later Nicolas Besnier, Claude Ballin and Thomas Germain, already 'Silversmiths to His Majesty' were appointed 'Sole silversmiths to His Majesty and his House', working each one year, Besnier for the remainder of 1723, Ballin for 1724 and Germain for 1725. It was laid down that each should finish any work he had already begun and that in case of need they should meet each evening to help one another. '*Le Roi veut et ordonne*' that they should enjoy all the advantages of this appointment and that they should describe themselves in all public and private documents 'Silversmiths to His Majesty', in virtue of which

Candlesticks and Candelabra

135 Pair of cluster column candlesticks, height 7 ins, by Pierre Masse, 1675
136 Pair of candlesticks, height 5½ ins, by Charles Delafond, 1680

138 Marks on candlestick in figure 137

137 One of a set of four candlesticks by Gilles Govel, 1719

139 One of a set of four candlesticks by Edmé-Pierre Balzac, 1740

140 Pair of candelabra with stems by François Riel, 1737, and branches by Jacques Duguay, 1739
141 Pair of candelabra by Louis Regnard, 1743

142 One of a pair of candelabra, height 13½ ins, by Jean-Baptiste-François Chéret, 1768-9
143 Pair of silver-gilt candelabra by Henry Auguste, 1788-9

Miscellaneous

144 Small, silver-mounted tobacco box by François Joubert, 1756-62

145 Left: Basin with shaving attachment by Jean Fauche, 1745-6, with chin-piece by Joseph-Pierre-Jacques Duguay, 1760-1, length 13 ins

146 Silver-gilt chalice and paten, maker's mark B P beneath a fleur-de-lis, mid 17th century

Designs for Silver

147 Title page of designs for silver by Masson

148 Meissonnier's portrait

149 Title page

150 Design for ice bucket, 1723
151 Monstrance made for a house of
Carmelite Nuns at Poitiers, 1727

152 Table centre and terrines, made for the
Duke of Kingston, 1735

153 'Nef pour le Roy'

154 Project for a
candelabra

155 Terrine with fish finial

156 Terrine with vegetable finial

157 Stand for salad-oil bottles

158 and 159 Design for
candlestick from two
angles, 1728

160 Design for the stem
of a candlestick

161 Three-branch
candelabra from
Meissonnier's design, by
Claude Duvivier, 1734-5
162 Marks on
candlestick

and in assurance of his good will, His Majesty has signed with his hand and caused to be countersigned.

Thomas Germain, now fifty-two, had arrived, and commissions began to reach him from abroad, notably a gold chalice for the Elector of Cologne, all trace of which seems to have been lost since 1795 during the French invasion. It was greatly admired by the Bavarian princes, nephews of the Elector, who visited Paris in November 1725 and saw the chalice when it was not quite finished. Again I quote from *Le Mercure*: 'This piece did this excellent master great honour and could satisfy the most delicate, subtle taste.' There followed numerous toilet services – one for the King of Portugal, then two years later another for the Princess of Brazil. Then, in 1728, another was designed and executed for the Queen of Spain, wife of Philip v, and in 1732 and 1733 two others, one for the King, the other for the Queen of the Two Sicilies, who also commissioned two cadenas and two gold *couverts*. In 1726 he delivered to Louis xv's Queen, Marie Leczinska, the day after her arrival in France, a notable toilet service of fifty-one pieces including twelve tall candlesticks, each of their stems formed by three caryatids and 'a knife to remove powder of which the blade is of gold and the handle enriched with diamonds and enamels'. As to the service for the Queen of the Two Sicilies, the only description which has survived is that of the chest which contained it: 'The exterior,' writes the invaluable *Mercure*, 'is decorated with gilded bronze and green velvet, enriched with gold, the whole in admirable taste. It is accompanied by a velvet cloth, cherry coloured, and beautifully embroidered with allegorical subjects pertaining to marriage.' Naturally, from 1725, his name appears regularly in the *Journal général du Garde-Meuble*. In 1725 he delivered an inkstand, a powder box and a sponge box in silver; two years later, in collaboration with Ballin, a little silver service (described as a *nécessaire*) of twenty-six pieces, engraved with the Royal Arms and three crowns, and later that year two sauce boats in gold, gondola-shaped, and a mustard pot with a shell-shaped cover. After every royal birth from 1726 until 1767 either Thomas Germain or his son François-Thomas provided a gold rattle for each successive child; less exalted children in France have made do with silver. Among his minor commissions was one from Marie Leczinska who happened to meet old Maréchal de Villars leaning on a wooden stick worth next to nothing. The Queen asked him to accept another and sent one of her gentlemen, a Monsieur Campan, to buy from Thomas Germain the finest stick in gold and enamels he could find. Campan duly presented the stick on the Queen's behalf to the Marshal who said he had nothing to offer the messenger in exchange but asked him to accept the old stick he used when in command of the army at Marchiennes and at Denain – a stick which was preserved in the Campan family until August 1792 when the Campan house at the entrance of the Tuileries was pillaged by the mob and partly burnt, and the stick thrown into the street as valueless.

Previous to 1728 the House of Braganza had dealt mainly with English silversmiths; in 1724, for instance, the King had ordered a silver bath from London weighing 900 marcs. But the reputation of Thomas Germain was by now firmly established and the Portuguese court became one of his most important foreign supporters, beginning with an order in 1728 for 6,000 marcs of silver objects and eight marcs of gold. In 1744 he made six gold crowns and a cross nine feet six inches high. There was also a complete service, already despatched to Lisbon at the time of his death and many other pieces. He had also received a commission for figures of the twelve apostles, receiving 10,000 livres as advance payment, but he was only able to finish the models. From the long list of the silver he provided for the French court during the 1730's and 40's the following must be taken as a mere sample.

An entire service for bedroom, table, chapel – seventy-nine pieces – for the Dauphin when a child. That was in 1736. Between 1740 and 1746 he provided all the silver necessary for the King's daughters, and in 1746 he made a complete service for the household of the newly-born daughter of the Dauphin, Marie-Thérèse. There are a surprising number of inkstands as the years pass – surprising, that is, until one remembers that when one of the royal cabinet-makers delivered a writing table or desk, a royal silversmith was automatically commissioned to make an inkstand for it. Moreover, the *Compagnie des Indes* was in the habit of presenting the King with a bureau at least once a year and this again meant another commission for the royal silversmiths.

Apart from the work Thomas Germain carried out for the French court and to the order of other Royalties, there were in addition the gifts which Louis xv made abroad, notably the various objects, including a silver table three feet and a half in diameter, which the King presented to the Sultan Mahmoud I in 1742 – their value was estimated at 237,960 livres according to the Archives of the French Foreign Office.

His last work for Louis xv was a pair of girandoles in gold, which, wrote his contemporary the Abbé Lambert in 1754, 'suffice to make his memory eternal'. They are described in detail in the *Journal du Garde-Meuble*: eighteen and a half inches in height, each in the form of a tree with foliage, four amours hanging a garland on the branches. Louis xv had them placed in his new winter room at Versailles, next to two sugar bowls, also gold, by Roëttiers. They were famous from the moment they were made and appear in all the inventories from 1767 until 1789. After that, there is no mention of them and there is no doubt that, like so much else, they were melted down after the Revolution to help re-establish the credit of the new born Republic during its first desperate years.

Few portraits of such men as Thomas Germain have survived the passage of more than two centuries – indeed, few people of his sort were painted at all, or, if they were, their likenesses have been lost in the limbo of unidentified portraits by minor artists. Germain, however, was painted by Nicolas de Largillière (1656-1746) and, to judge by the superb double portrait of the silversmith and his wife belonging to the Gulbenkian Foundation in Lisbon, the two, painter and silversmith must surely have been on terms of close friendship (Figure 163). Thomas and his wife, Anne-Denise Gauchelet, are dressed in their ordinary clothes, Germain with one hand on a great silver vase, and with the other pointing to other designs on a shelf. Largillière, upon whom had descended much of the panache of Van Dyck, thanks partly to his early years in Antwerp, and partly to his association for some time with Van Dyck's pupil, Peter Lely, in London, could when he chose make grandees look like supercilious demigods, but here he is working in the intimacy of his subjects' lodgings in the Louvre and shows us two workaday people, the one proud of his skill, the other no less proud of her husband's fame: altogether a most sympathetic performance.

Various other commissions came to Germain from his connection with the Paris Municipality, first as councillor, then as *échevin*, an office which, under the *ancien régime*, combined the duties of magistrate with that of responsibility for the police. There is no exact equivalent but one might perhaps equate it with that of sheriff or alderman. Apart from the inevitable presents to visiting princes or grandees – inkstands for instance – there were several ex-voto gifts to one or other Paris church. Among the latter was a famous hanging lamp for the Abbey of St Geneviève, a gift from the Paris Municipality to commemorate the saint's intercession on behalf of the inhabitants which at last put an end to the six months' frost which had so cruelly tried the people during the previous winter. This was in 1740. An earlier and a secular masterpiece was the gold sword which the City of Paris decided to present to the Dauphin, then aged five years, in 1734. This was an entrancing toy, 'worked with great delicacy and in proportion to the recipient's age'. It was presented to him, accompanied with many compliments; it is not surprising to learn that the child was more delighted by the sword than by the speeches. In 1779 it was still in the Garde-Meuble – by the time of the Revolution it had disappeared. As to the hanging lamp, this was unfinished at Thomas Germain's death, was modified and completed by his son, François-Thomas, and presented in 1754.

In 1748, when he was sixty-five, he had a seizure and died, the victim, it was said at the time, of a macabre and dotty dispute between the two sides of the medical profession. His physician prescribed bleeding, but his surgeon refused to carry out the physician's instructions; his not to reason why but to uphold the honour of his branch of the science of healing. The body of Thomas Germain was buried in the church of St Louis-du-Louvre, which he had designed and which had been consecrated in 1744. He had given his services free and had made a handsome contribution towards the cost.

His contemporaries had no doubts as to his importance. J. F. Blondel in his *Architecture Française*, 1754, writes thus: 'There is not a European Court which does not possess work in silver by this great man. He took so much pains that more than once he began something afresh, because his workpeople, although he chose the most skilful available, had scamped some portion. To the talents for his profession which he had received from nature, Germain added a profound knowledge of design, of sculpture and of architecture.' The Abbé Lambert is no less enthusiastic, 'The reader will doubtless be surprised that the life of this great man could be sufficient for so great a number of works; one will be still more surprised to learn that he would allow nothing to appear which was not his own composition and which he had not designed, modelled and chased himself.'

Mariette finds him the finest silversmith in France since Ballin and superior to Meissonier. Forty years after the death of Germain, J. M. Lecain, Warden of the Silversmiths Guild, paid this tribute to his predecessor in the *Encylopédie Méthodique des Arts et Métiers Mécaniques*:

Claude Ballin, silversmith to Louis XIV, executed for this prince superb pieces of silver furniture which were melted down at the time of the Peace of Riswick [sic]. He had for successor Pierre Germain, who was also silversmith to the King; but most remarkable of all was the latter's son, Thomas Germain. This artist was the creator of beautiful silver work which will serve for ever as models for the future. It is then only right to render to this illustrious man, to this inestimable artist the tribute of the praises which are his due. It is inconceivable that the portrait or the bust of so great a man, in his capacity as artist and past-warden, is not in the hall of the guild.

Finally there is the tribute of Lempereur in his *Dictionnaire des Artistes*:

Germain could invent easily and without repeating himself. His taste for ornament is pure and wise; his forms are agreeable, rich and elegant without being tormented and his execution is such that the work of the chasing-tool disappears and one perceives only the nature and true character of the object. Wholly occupied with his art and all that concerned it, he neglected everything else and did not make a fortune proportionate to merit and the length of time he spent on his work. It should be the duty of the great ones of the earth to right the wrong an exceptional man does to himself by his noble passion to excel ; they could do this by recognising the fact that they grant favours to frivolous or dangerous talents.

François-Thomas Germain (1726-91)

François-Thomas, fourth son of Thomas Germain, found himself at the age of twenty-two an accomplished silversmith thanks to the training he had received from his father, the heir to that great craftsman's reputation, to much unfinished work and to very little working capital. The latter deficiency, added to his own ambitions and extravagance, was destined to bring him to disaster; meanwhile few men could have begun their professional careers under fairer auspices. A few months before his death Thomas asked the King to allow him to leave his lodging in the Louvre in favour of his son. The Royal consent was dated 1 March 1748 and at the same time François-Thomas was enrolled as the Royal silversmith and admitted Master of the Guild, his mark similar to that of his father, F.T.G. and a fleece. The young man's first task was inevitably to finish several objects which were still in the workshop, among them a second chalice for the Archbishop of Cologne, a magnificent work, according to the Duc de Luynes, of which the gold cost 15,000 livres, the fashioning 35,000 livres. In 1752 he was entrusted with the making of the elaborate presents the King sent to the 'Nabab of Golconda' [? The Nizam of Hyderabad] which included some silver-gilt tureens surmounted by all kinds of vegetables in the fashion of the day which, said the enthusiastic *Mercure de France*, 'seems to dispute with the produce of nature'. He began also the long series of silver wares, from inkstands to altar vessels, for the various members of the royal family which made him famous in his own right, not merely as his father's son, and which led to a multitude of commissions from abroad, such as candlesticks in 1765 for the King of Poland and in the following year an *escritoire* in the form of an antique vase, at each side two children, an eagle above.

But his most famous and elaborate work was that commissioned by the Courts of Russia and Portugal. The first of the Russian orders appears to have been for three centrepieces for the Empress Elizabeth as a present to her uncle Prince Soltikoff, victor in 1759 at Kumersdorf over Frederick the Great; Bacchus and l'Amour and, at one end a little girl, at the other a little boy with two doves. The second was formed as an Amor making music, the third as a little girl playing with doves. They descended from the Soltikoff family to that of Miatlieff and were later purchased by the Czar.

Other commissions were for a whole table service, a famous mirror surmounted by the Crown and Russian coat of arms, each side with Amors holding flower garlands, and a silver-gilt toilet service. There were, of course, commissions to other French silversmiths also, notably the service made for Count Orloff by Roëttiers. After Germain's bankruptcy his place was taken in Imperial favour by Henry Auguste who executed many commissions for Catherine the Great, among them a toilet service for Count Bobrinskoy.

Meanwhile the King of Portugal, no less than his brother of France, accepted François-Thomas as the natural and inevitable successor of his father. There was a kettle and basin for the Royal medicine cupboard, the kettle ornamented with a figure of Aesculapius, his hat providing the cover, while the basin had a swan at one end, a cock at the other. In 1757 he was commissioned, in collaboration with Jacques Ballin, to repair all the plate belonging to the Court, and in 1766 L'Avant-Coureur describes a gold déjeuner he made for the King and a silver-gilt toilet service for the Princess. In 1765 he had four table services in course of manufacture in his workshop, also for Portugal, and in 1774 a silver-gilt toilet service, a déjeuner, a nécessaire of gold, four dozen plates, three dozen complete table sets, three dozen silver-gilt knives and a gold sword. Altogether the plate made by François-Thomas for the account of Portugal alone added up more than three thousand pieces, many of the most elaborate description.

These royal commissions from three separate courts, neither of which worried overmuch about expenditure, not to mention work for numerous private individuals scarcely less extravagant, would, on the face of it, have ensured a distinguished and prosperous career. But Germain, unlike his sober, plain-living father and grandfather, was always in debt and did not make things any easier, according to contemporary reports, by keeping expensive mistresses. But gossip would seem to have exaggerated the extent of his escapades. It is true that he became enamoured of a dancer at the Italian Comedy, Mlle. Hughes, and no doubt she cost him a fair amount for a time, but she soon deserted him for a richer man, M. de Rochemaure, a naval officer. The industrious Germain Bapst dug out this story from the Journal des Inspecteurs de M. de Sartine, Brussels, 1863 under the date 14 August 1762; the Inspector comments drily: 'This was a much more profitable acquaintance.'

Deserting the stage, Germain then ran off with Mlle. Maisonville, the daughter of a rag-and-bone merchant, and set her up in the Rue Neuve-St-Eustache, but as he only gave her ten louis per month plus her dresses, this affair could scarcely have brought him to a deficiency of two and a half millions. The Police Inspector clearly approved of Mlle. Maisonville, for the entry of 1 July 1763 reads: 'She is tall, well-made, skin and throat admirable and is endowed with a very interesting face.' However, this attachment presumably came to an end fairly soon, for it was in that year he married Marguerite Le Sieurre Desbrières who brought with her a dowry of eighty thousand livres. By the beginning of 1765 the dowry and the modest thirty thousand livres he had inherited from his father had disappeared and he was more than two million, four hundred thousand livres in the red. His bankruptcy entailed his giving up the apartment in the Louvre, and the remainder of his days were spent in a spider's web of legal complexities too tedious to unravel in a book of this nature. He continued to work, of course, and many of his best pieces date from the years between 1765 and about 1780. After that, next to nothing is heard of him. His creditors and even his friends accused him of concealing the true state of his affairs. This may be true to some extent, but the basic reason for his fall must be found in his temperament. He was an able craftsman with no business sense, justly proud of his skill and convinced that the world would be bound eventually to honour so conspicuous a talent in good hard cash – as indeed it does nearly two centuries after his death.

Largillière's most sympathetic portrait of Thomas Germain and his wife is illustrated in Figure 163, with a pair of candelabra from the Firestone Collection by Thomas, dated 1732-3, which are clearly modelled from the single candelabra to which he is pointing (Figure 164). The great ewer upon which his right hand, holding a graving tool, is resting is not likely to have survived. These are exceptional pieces though not so elaborate as the great *surtout* (table centrepiece) which follows with its reclining hounds at each end and the wholly charming reclining cupid on the lid (Figure 165). This is of exceptional importance because the silver made by Thomas Germain for the Portuguese court before his death in 1748 was apparently all destroyed by the Lisbon earthquake of 1755. His son François-Thomas was commissioned to replace it, and evidently made use of this centrepiece by his father which bears the mark of Thomas Germain and the Paris date letter for 1730-1 and also the son's usual inscription on his important pieces, *Fait par F.-T. Germain sculp. orf du Roy aux Galleries du Louvre à Paris 1757*.

That Thomas could work with equal facility and grace on a smaller scale is shown by the little pot on the table in the double portrait by Largillière and by the two-branch candelabra of 1747 with its shaft for a shade in the Louvre (Figure 166). Also from the Louvre and by Thomas Germain is the salt of 1734-6 (Figure 167), playful, amusing, and oddly dignified (if a turtle can ever be dignified) but without any pretty rococo asymmetrical tricks which can be so charming when carried out by, or to the designs of a considerable talent. The salt by François-Thomas Germain from the Lisbon Museum (1764-5) (Figure 168) can be usefully compared with this turtle confection.

It is the fashion rather to belittle the reputation of the junior Germain (I suspect quite unconsciously) because he was a trifle scatty and went bankrupt. A success story strikes the imagination, failure makes one feel uncomfortable; a good many of his contemporaries lost money because of him, and in consequence he had a bad press. But, in the context of his time and by comparison with the works of any of his contemporaries and rivals (the two Roëttiers, for instance) it is surely difficult to find fault with his work even though the world of today is not invariably *en rapport* with the richness and intricacy of his designs. Fantasy, particularly in such a piece as the salt mentioned above, with its shell *motif* supported by two fish and with various crustacea scattered around apparently haphazard on cover and base, is ridden with a loose rein, but the rider is fully in control. By contrast the rectangular dish and cover with rounded corners, 1757-8 (Figure 169), has a basic gravity about it – but a gravity which is redeemed from solemnity by the delicious overlapping leaf design of the cover, with its twisted stalk for a finial.

Opinions no doubt will differ as to the complete success of the other salt from the Lisbon Museum, not that it is not gaily ingenious, the two little Indian boys exactly in balance as they hold up the leafy vegetable above their heads – there is an easy fluidity about this design which would make criticism difficult were it not that this sort of thing, when carried out in porcelain, seems more satisfactory (Figure 170). Perhaps it is the fact that the two children are supporting something instead of merely resting on something which provokes a certain feeling of uneasiness as one looks at this piece.

No such criticism can be levelled at the centrepiece or the two tureens with their stands which follow. The three-piece table-centre (*surtout*) from the Gulbenkian Foundation is shown in two photographs (Figures 171 and 172), one of them the centre portion only, and it can only be described as ravishing – the two little Amors squabbling together upon a rocky mound scattered with bunches of grapes, a boy and a girl as two separate figures *en suite*, the date 1763-4. With the two splendid tureens, each on its stand, one is on fairly familiar princely ground. There are slight differences of detail; in each case there are two children beneath the handles, and two children playing with a goat

164 Pair of three-light candelabra by Thomas Germain, 1732-3
165 Centrepiece by Thomas Germain, 1730-1, signed also by F.-T. Germain, 1757

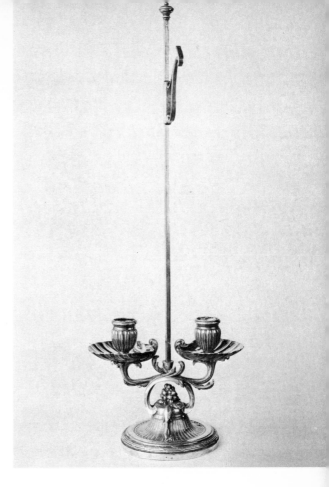

166 Candelabra by Thomas
Germain, 1747-8

167 Salt-cellar by Thomas Germain, 1734-6

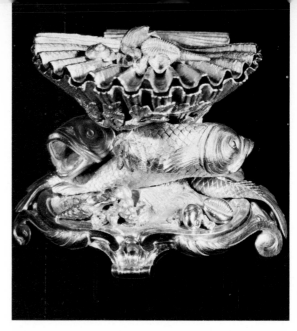

168 Salt-cellar by François-Thomas Germain, 1764-5

169 Rectangular dish and cover by François-Thomas Germain 1757-8

170 Salt-cellar by François-Thomas Germain, 1757-8

171 Complete three-piece table-centre by François-Thomas Germain, 1763-4
172 Central figure of table-centre

173 One of four terrines by François-Thomas Germain, 1756-7

174 Terrine and stand by François-Thomas Germain, 1756-7

175 Terrine, height 32 cm, by François-Thomas Germain, 1758-9
176 Marks on terrine

177 Pair of silver-gilt salvers, diameter 31 cm, by François-Thomas Germain, 1757
178 Mark of F.-T. Germain

ELEMENTS

D'ORFEVRERIE

DIVISÉS

En deux Parties de Cinquante
Feuilles Chacune
Composés par PIERRE

GERMAIN

Marchand Orfevre Joaillier

A PARIS

PREMIERE PARTIE

Le Prix est de

12^{tt}

SE VENDENT

A Paris chez L'Auteur place du Carousel
à L'Orfevrerie du ROY

M·DCC·XLVIII·

auec priuilege du Roy

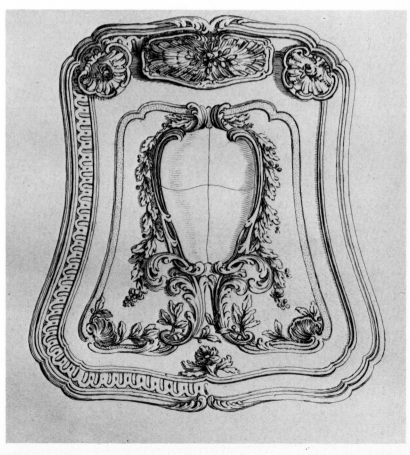

180 Design
for terrine

181 Design
for cadenas

182 One of seven designs by Jacques Roëttiers, included in Germain's book

183 Design for candlestick by G. M. Moser, R.A.

above. The stands appear to be identical. Each tureen is one of a set of four, their date 1756-7, and they are as fine examples of mid-eighteenth century French silver as exists anywhere in the world (Figures 173 and 174).

One other splendid tureen and stand, also by F.-T. Germain – the stand identical with the others – has the same two children at each end beneath the handles which are formed by swirling folded cloths which they hold above their heads; the finial two children, one of them protecting a dove from a dog. This is one of the many pieces of French silver commissioned by the Russian Court and now in the Hermitage at Leningrad. The base bears both Germain's inscription and the mark for 1758-9, and also the Russian mark for 1762 (Figures 175 and 176).

By December 1756 Germain is said to have been employing one hundred and twenty workmen on four great services for the King of Portugal, and actually completed three of them. With the fourth he got as far as 'forty-eight silver-gilt plates and thirty-six *couverts*'. When the Portuguese court fled to Brazil at the time of Napoleon's invasion of the Peninsula, this vast amount of plate went with it, to be divided up when Brazil became independent. The second and last Emperor of Brazil, Dom Pedro II, was forced to abdicate, and whatever pieces of French silver engraved with the arms of the House of Braganza have appeared from time to time can be traced back to this South American source. The half which returned to Portugal when Brazil declared itself independent remained in the various Royal palaces until the fall of the monarchy in 1910, and since then, with few exceptions, has been displayed in the Lisbon Museum.

But there is one work by F.-T. Germain, not in Lisbon but which was acquired by Mr Stavros Niarchos with the Puiforcat Collection, which some of us regard as a finer thing than any of his more elaborate centre-pieces. This is the pair of silver-gilt salvers of Figure 177. In the centre they are engraved with the arms of the House of Braganza within delicate wreaths of laurel, and their borders are formed of branches of celery entwined by six alternate designs of palmettes, vine leaves, grapes and (most unusually) coffee berries. The result is a ravishing harmony of balance and movement. If everything else by the son of the admittedly great Thomas had disappeared, these two salvers alone would place him in the front rank among the silversmiths of his generation. They bear the marks for 1756-7 and also his customary inscription with the date 1757 (Figure 178).

Pierre Germain II, known as 'the Roman' (1716-83)

There was another Pierre Germain, who was also a Paris silversmith, who used to be confused with the elder of the famous family. If he was related in any way it was at some considerable distance. Very little of his work has been identified and, apart from a toilet service made by him for the Princess of the Asturias designed by Caffieri, he appears to have made no great mark. No one knows how the sobriquet 'the Roman' became attached to him. He was apprenticed in 1736 to the well-known Nicolas Besnier, silversmith to the King with lodgings in the Louvre, and was admitted Master in 1744. He served as Warden in the Guild on several occasions and at his death was honoured by a memorial service at the church of St Eloi. He is, however, famous as the author of *Eléments d'Orfèvrerie* which he published from his house on the Place du Carrousel in 1748 (Figures 179-182). This consists of one hundred and five pages of plates, nearly all signed by him; there are also seven signed by the celebrated Jean-Jacques Roëttiers. They provide a practical guide to the style in vogue at the time and nothing could be more delightful than his modest introduction:

I have only one aim in composing this work—to encourage young people .... It is not my intention to lay down definite rules ....
I hope no one will disapprove of this work—I have only wished to help young people. I have added some designs of silver by Monsieur Roëttiers which at the moment he is executing for Monsieur le Dauphin. I shall be happy if my efforts find favour and contribute to the perfection of those who wish to embrace this profession.

His designs are less elaborate and, on the whole, more down to earth than those of Meissonnier. The same can scarcely be said for one of the seven designed by Roëttiers in the same book – a charming thing but, as far as is known, never actually executed (Figure 182).

The final illustration in this section is of a drawing by George Michael Moser, RA (1709-83), a Founder Member of the Royal Academy and its first Keeper in 1768. His indebtedness to current French fashions is evident (Figure 183).

66

From the Distant Past to the 19th Century

It is possible to appreciate French or any other silver without paying overmuch attention to the marks. On the other hand, style alone is by no means an absolutely safe guide, and the more the amateur becomes interested in the subject, the more likely he is to consult Nocq and Carré from time to time – and very rewarding he will find them. While the marks on the pieces illustrated here have been given the attention they deserve, they have not been allowed to assume undue importance; we are dealing with works of art, not just stamps. At the same time, for a proper understanding of the manner in which the trade was organised, some kind of historical survey is required and what follows is an attempt to explain as simply as possible how the craft grew to the proportions it did. If that is to be done, the system of marking, however boring some may find it and however complicated it may seem, must at least be described in outline.

The Guild System

The earliest written record of the regulations governing the trades of Paris was compiled by Etienne Boileau, Provost of the City in 1260. In it he sets out the rules observed by the goldsmiths – the word covers all workers in precious metals – and these rules were the basis of all subsequent developments. They were amended from time to time by royal decree, and were codified, as were the regulations for many other crafts, under Louis xiv in 1679. These regulations remained unaltered in essentials until the Revolution of 1789. They were broadly similar to the rules which experience found necessary in other countries and grew naturally enough beneath the shelter of the mediaeval guild which, while protecting the interests of its members, also preserved reasonable standards. It was the duty of, say brewers and bakers, to ensure that beer or bread was not adulterated.

Because gold and silver were metals of intrinsic value and of immense importance to the government, the Crown was in due course compelled to take an interest if only to ensure that the coins were not clipped and the surplus sold for fashioning, but until 1543 the king did not exercise any formal control. Previously it had been left to the Guild, but in that year Francis I made one system obligatory for the whole of France. The trade was still administered by the various Guilds in the chief towns, but from that moment the Crown was in a position to supervise – and, needless to add, to improve its always languishing finances by one tax or another.

All the evidence goes to show that, by the fifteenth century, there was an extraordinary amount of domestic silver in daily use. In 1465 the Chancellor of the States-General of Tours, Juvenal des Ursins, is said to have declared that one could meet no one in France who did not claim to eat off silver. Jean de Saint-Gelais wrote that under Charles VIII one could scarcely enter a workman's house throughout the country without finding silver vessels. One can take these and similar claims with several grains of salt, but they do indicate the trend of fashion. Coming to more modern times, a decree of Louis XIII in 1629 denounced the use of precious metal for humble domestic household utensils, from which it is reasonable to assume that by the seventeenth century, in great houses at least, even kitchen ware was frequently made from silver rather than from pewter. As regal extravagance and currency troubles became worse Louis XIV's advisers found it necessary to introduce sumptuary laws on three separate occasions, in 1689, 1700 and 1709, the King himself setting an example by sending to the Mint his silver furniture. This was in 1689. The 1709 decree was even more drastic – courtiers were bidden to give up all their silver and to eat off earthenware. This was a godsend to the struggling faïence industry, but still left a great deal of silver in private hands. Saint-Simon sheds an entertaining side-light upon the operation: 'Top people in the capital,' he says, 'who dared not disobey and a few others who believed they would obtain some advantage, swam with the current. There were no others in Paris, and practically no one in the provinces. I admit that I was the rearguard. When I saw I was almost the only one of my rank eating off silver I sent about a thousand pistoles worth to the Mint and locked up the rest.' A sour comment on the passion of the people of Paris to put their money into silver plate was provided in 1745 by a report to the Crown's Controller of Finance: 'Parisians love silver plate and collect it in preference to acquiring income from investments as do people in the Provinces.' These sumptuary laws, which obviously, in spite of Saint-Simon, resulted in the destruction of great quantities of plate, were not in any way due to a puritanical dislike of display but to economic theory, which laid down that the wealth of a nation consisted in the amount of gold and silver currency in circulation, without which it was considered commerce could not flourish.

This theory, which was a general belief of the time, found definite expression in the preamble to the edict of 1689. Gold and silver must be converted into money, was the gist of this formidable document, and must not be allowed to lie idle in the form of plate. Individuals were so fond of vessels of gold and silver that a currency famine was paralysing trade and the mints (*Hotels de la Frappe*) were starved. But long before the theory had found its way into other official documents; in 1579, for instance, an edict of Henri III put a tax on goldsmiths' work, ostensibly to 'punish luxury', in fact to raise revenue and to prevent sumptuous pieces of plate being locked away 'more by curiosity than necessity – which is a piece of dead gold or silver from which one derives no profit'. But this tax does not appear to have accomplished much, for in 1631 we read of another edict, again ostensibly devised to restrain individual expenditure on luxuries, and clapping a tax on plate. The Paris silversmiths paid 24,000 livres to the Treasury, and the king revoked the tax two years later. The Government, having tasted blood, put on a new tax in 1642; once again the silversmiths paid up, this time 30,000 livres, in return for a promise that such a tax should never be imposed again – a promise which was kept for thirty years; many other governments in many other parts of the world have interpreted the word 'perpetuity' in a less generous manner. Times change, new crises arise, and what seemed reasonable in one year has become contrary to public policy in the next. The year 1672 was a turning point. A tax (*Le Droit de Marque*) was finally established, the edict once again criticising the luxury of gold and silver articles 'which considerably diminishes trade among our subjects, for trade can only be carried on with an abundance of money in circulation'. The silversmiths protested that the tax should be paid only when the object was sold and not immediately it was made. That sounds reasonable but the Government thought otherwise – and in 1674 doubled the tax. Other impositions, too numerous to mention in detail here, followed, until in March 1791 the National Assembly abolished all indirect taxation – only to re-establish the *Droit de Marque* in September.

The temptation to circumvent the taxgatherer is endemic in the human race, and it is not surprising to read that certain of the weaker brethren succumbed. The penalties for forging the marks of the various persons who farmed the taxes were severe, at least on paper. In the edict of 1681, the wrongdoer was threatened with a fine of 3,000 livres, five years in the galleys, even a life sentence for a second offence. In 1724, after some serious frauds, the death penalty was introduced though it seems to have been carried out on only one occasion in 1753, when an engraver was hanged for forging marks. Richard Jarry, convicted in 1736 for possessing spoons and forks bearing false marks of the tax farmer, was more fortunate. He was condemned to do penance, bare-footed in his shirt, a cord round his neck, at the doors of Notre-Dame, with a placard front and back with the legend : 'Working silversmith using false marks', and to confess his crime in a loud voice and 'ask pardon of God, ourselves and Justice', and then to be hanged, *in effigy* [my italics], in the Place de Grêve.

In his compilation of 1260 Boileau recorded that the standard of silver used by French goldsmiths had to be at least equal to the English sterling – that is, 925 parts of pure silver to 1,000. In 1549, it was fixed at 958 to 1,000, with a permitted tolerance of two grains (or 7/1,000) on each side; in the pre-Revolution weights-and-measures system this high standard was recorded as 11 deniers 12 grains, and the 1789 *Almanach des Monnaies* shows that nearly all the towns of France were working to this standard. The exceptions were Lille; the two towns in the Franche-Comté, Besançon and Salins (11 deniers 8 grains), and Strasbourg, which got along happily enough on the very low standard of 9 deniers 20 grains; though all occasionally used the Paris standard, but in that case the pieces bore an additional mark. Avignon alone, which belonged to the Pope, took no notice of French regulations; it used either of two standards, 9 deniers or 11 deniers 10 grains, but as the few Avignon goldsmiths were not compelled to have their work assayed, it is, to say the least, unlikely that they paid very much attention.

The Guild regulations as eventually codified and brought up to date in 1679 were summarised in 1734 by one of the Paris Wardens, Paul Leroy, and applied in principle, if not wholly in practice, throughout France. First came a lengthy apprenticeship of eight years in a master's workshop, and then two or three as a journeyman. The young man could then apply to be admitted as Master, but he frequently found himself in difficulties, for the number of goldsmiths in each town Guild was fixed by royal decree and it was necessary to wait for a vacancy. In any case he had to pass an examination by the Wardens in both practice and theory of the craft, and he had also to satisfy them that he was a person of integrity. Finally, he had to produce a 'masterpiece', a *chef d'oeuvre*, in the Wardens' presence, generally a fairly simple object which would not take too long to make. It is recorded that, in their respective tests, Jean Brissot made a cup in about five hours, Jean Petit a covered salt, and Robert-Joseph Auguste a spoon and fork. Once he had survived all this, the candidate would be presented by the Wardens to the officials of the Mint who would ask him further questions; one would imagine that this final hurdle would not be over-difficult to negotiate. He would then take the oath, promising to abide by the regulations, and his sponsor would hand over a sum of money as security (*caution*), which in Paris by the eighteenth century was 1,000 livres.

(The English phrase 'caution-money' is still in use at our older universities.) The next step was for the candidate to register his mark. This was struck on two copper plates, one of which was kept at the Mint, the other at the Guild Hall. Finally the Wardens entered his name in the register as a duly qualified fledgling goldsmith and silversmith, with a description of his mark. In addition, from the end of the eighteenth century, the mark was printed in candlesoot in the margin of the register. A little reflection will be sufficient to detect a serious flaw in this theoretically admirable arrangement – the fact that Masters were limited in numbers. This must have been extremely frustrating for ambitious and competent young men, and while what has been described above remained the normal series of fences the aspirant had to surmount, means were gradually devised to circumvent them. For instance, if there had been some failure on his part to serve the whole of his apprenticeship, he could apply to the Crown for letters patent to give him the right to practise his craft. Several eminent silversmiths became Masters in this way, among them Robert-Joseph Auguste and J. H. Vancombert. Then sons of practising silversmiths seem to have been spared a formal apprenticeship because it was taken for granted that their fathers would automatically give them proper training, though, like everyone else, they had to pass the usual tests and fashion their masterpiece. The Guild, though for a time only, also made a concession to the widow of a Master, receiving her as a member and thus enabling her to carry on her husband's business. A very special registration was reserved for the young craftsmen who taught their skill to children at the Hôpital de la Trinité, a foundling hospital, established by Francis I in 1545. Two only were allowed to teach at this institution at any one time and, after serving eight years, they were rewarded in this manner. But the real breach in the rigid set of rules which the Guild had erected for itself came in 1608, when Henri IV set aside a group of workshops on the ground floor of the Louvre, beneath the Long Gallery, in which specially chosen painters, cabinet-makers and other artists, including goldsmiths and silversmiths, could work without reference to their guilds. It was an enormously valuable privilege and at first sight would seem to mark the inevitable end of any reasonable control, for the Wardens had no right of inspection. But all the available evidence appears to show that though the trade was divided in this way between those enjoying royal protection and those who did not, the advantage of working under royal patronage was such that no one thus honoured would dream of departing from the high standard expected of him, and in any case such appointments were not made without careful previous consideration. Not unnaturally, there was considerable jealousy on the part of those who had become Masters in the ordinary way. In addition to these Court appointments there were a few other silver-smiths who were attached to certain royal households and so enjoyed similar privileges.

Having surmounted these various hurdles and registered his mark the newly fledged Master could open shop without delay. If his mastership had been obtained in Paris, he could work elsewhere if he wished, provided there was a vacancy in whatever district he chose; he merely had to register at the office of the local Guild. An interesting point is that he *had* to practise; if he took a prolonged holiday or closed down he had to turn his mark into the Guild. Obviously, with a limited membership – in Paris during the eighteenth century the limit was fixed at 500 – there would be no profit in the Guild carrying passengers, who would merely be keeping out eager and competent youngsters. For the whole of his professional life the silversmith (with the exceptions already noted) was under the control of the Wardens. Any dispute could be referred to the Paris Court of the Mint. His other troubles he shared with his fellow citizens, namely the demands of the tax-gatherer – in his case, a very special arrangement unlike anything known by his neighbours north of the Channel.

In Paris, the Wardens of the Guild were elected annually. There were five junior Wardens (*Jeunes Gardes*) who served for five years and one senior Warden (*Ancien Garde*) who served for one year. Consecutive terms were not allowed. Like new masters the Wardens had to swear to carry out their duties faithfully before the officers of the Mint, and their marks had to be registered at both the Guild Hall and at the Mint.

The Guild Hall was known as *La Maison Commune*, and its mark as *Poinçon de la Commune*, or *Poinçon de la Communauté*. It was the Wardens who carried out the assay, examined the candidates for membership, destroyed goods which were not up to standard, inspected the workshops and were generally responsible for good conduct and discipline – very much as were their opposite numbers in other countries using not dissimilar methods of control but living in different circumstances. In Paris, the goldsmiths and silversmiths were to be found mostly on the Ile de la Cité and in shops on the Pont du Change and the Pont St Michel, with their Guildhouse and Chapel in the Rue des Orfèvres.

The Tax Farmers

The French system of collecting taxes under the *ancien régime* was to farm them out. The right, or perhaps one might say the duty to collect a particular tax or taxes, was leased to individuals who paid over an agreed sum to the Treasury and then, for the period of their agreement, made as much as they could out of the operation. Until 1672 the silver-smith was able to carry on his business without a specific tax being levied on his product. True, there had been a few attempts to levy a duty on gold and silver according to weight, but these came to nothing. But once Louis xiv and his Ministers had devised the *Droit de Marque* or Mark Duty, ostensibly to discourage the conversion of silver into plate for the economic reasons already explained, but also as a means of raising revenue, the trade found itself in the hands of a succession of tax farmers and did not escape until 1774. In that year the whole tax organisation was revised, not to be changed until the Revolution of 1789. Meanwhile the Farmer-General who had bought the right to collect all indirect taxes would generally, and especially between the years 1698 and 1756, sublet his right to collect the Mark Duty to an under-farmer (*Sous-Fermier du Droit de Marque*) for from five to seven years. This man would himself, through his subordinates, collect the tax in Paris itself and perhaps in a few other towns where the revenue might be worth his trouble, and sublease the other districts; and these minor farmers would sometimes hire off part of their domain to yet smaller men. Altogether a fairly elaborate pyramid of responsibility, which certainly paid the man at the top handsomely, without probably benefiting the revenue as much as might have been wished.

The system meant, of course, that all silver had to be marked not only with the maker's mark and Wardens' mark to guarantee it was by an admitted Master and was up to standard, but a mark or marks to show that the tax on each individual piece had been paid. These marks were the Charge and Discharge Marks. At first only completed work was marked, but from 1677 both charge and discharge marks became obligatory.

It is clear therefore that the number of marks one can expect to find on a piece of French silver is four, and generally in this order:

    1.   Maker's mark.
    2.   Wardens' mark.
    3.   Charge mark.
    4.   Discharge mark.

Occasionally there will be more, as for instance when a piece has been laid aside to be finished a few years later when there may perhaps be a new warden and a new farmer. As in England, makers, in addition to their initials, were fond of using a device as a mark, which was a play upon their names. Jacques Delavigne chose a vine leaf, Louis Regnard a fox, J.-P. Marteau a hammer, Jean du Moulin a windmill, and a son would often adopt the device used by his father; for instance, François-Thomas Germain took over the fleece used as mark by his father,

Thomas Germain. A widow often kept the device of her husband, adding her initials and a V for *veuve*, although the 1679 regulations laid down that she must not use a personal mark but have pieces from her workshop stamped by another silversmith – an edict which does not appear to have been very strictly enforced.

Although, speaking generally, the whole of the French gold and silver *Mistery* (to use the mediaeval English term) was controlled from Paris, there were exceptions. Certain provinces and towns acquired by the Crown after 1543 were exempt from the *Droit de Marque* – that is, Alsace, Lorraine, Franche-Comté, Rousillon, Béarn, Flanders and Hainault. Avignon, which belonged to the Papacy, was a law unto itself, and was not technically a part of France until the Revolution of 1789. There was also the Principality of Doubes, the property of the Bourbon family: this small area did not come directly under the crown until 1779. Consequently there was no charge and discharge mark in any of these territories; instead there was a recognition mark (*Poinçon de Reconnaissance*) which was merely to show the place of manufacture.

The system by which the *Droit de Marque* was collected by a multitude of under-farmers throughout the country, whose terms of office varied, resulted in so much inefficiency that even the easy-going administration of Louis xv at long last found that reform of some kind was essential and so, in 1774, both Farmer-General and under-farmers were abolished; instead all indirect taxes, including those on gold and silver, were to be collected by the *Régie* which had previously dealt only with direct taxes. A single official, the *Régisseur*, was appointed to collect the *Droit de Marque*, and the number of Mints was reduced from thirty-two to twenty-six. From 1775 until the Revolution the same charge and discharge marks were used throughout the area covered by each local mint, all of them engraved in Paris on a circular plaque, duplicates of which were circulated to the various mints.

Post-Revolution Silver Marks

In the first fine careless rapture of the 1789 Revolution the Guild System was abolished (March 1791) but within a month the Constituent Assembly re-established the Guild of the Goldsmiths and Silversmiths though Wardens seem to have exercised little or no control. No Wardens' mark has been found later than 1789. Instead a mark which has been called 'the unofficial assay mark' – a head of Apollo – was in use between 1793 and 1797, apparently because, though there was no legal requirement, Paris silversmiths felt that, because of complaints that silver was being sold below standard, they had better devise means of showing that they were not departing from honest traditions. However the Government tackled the problem seriously and sensibly in 1797. The Guilds were suppressed, restrictions were abolished. All a man had to do was to register his mark and open his shop. New marks were devised, each type covering the whole of France, in place of the multitudinous varieties under the old regime, and all work manufactured during the past few years had to be stamped afresh. Makers' marks were in the form of a lozenge and included his initials and device. Naturally, crowned fleur-de-lis, so frequently used in the past, had to go as symbolising the abolished monarchy.

The abolition of the Guilds threw the responsibility for the assay on to the state which, as previously, though now directly, levied a tax, and a single tax mark (*Poinçon de Guarantie*) replaced the former tax farmers' charge and discharge marks. Rather oddly, two standards were established; one 950/1,000 pure silver; the second, the low proportion of 800/1,000.

In 1798 a census was taken of all goldsmiths' and silversmiths' stocks to ensure that pre-Revolution pieces had been correctly marked; thanks to various frauds a similar check was undertaken in 1809 and again in 1819 and 1838.

New marks were devised in 1809 and there was a further revision in 1819. It was at that time that anvil marks were introduced – that is, the anvil on which the piece was placed for a mark to be struck was engraved with various insects, so that when the mark was punched on to a piece on one side an insect mark would appear on the reverse. The last major revision of the system took place in 1838, when the assay and excise marks were combined into a single mark, which is still in use.

Influence Beyond the Borders of France

While it is not necessary to take literally the disapproving statement of the Archbishop of Rheims in 1468 that there was scarcely a person in the country who did not eat off silver, there is ample evidence to show that, apart from the immense amount of vessels, reliquaries, crosses and statues in the churches, important people, from the monarch downwards, owned and used an imposing quantity of domestic plate. King Charles V, for instance, owned 906 pieces of plate weighing well over 30,000 ounces, one of them a plain gold cup shaped like a chalice weighing 22 ounces; his father, Jean II, had a golden throne, a chair overlaid with silver, and a magnificent series of table-fountains, nefs, aquamaniles and ewers. The Duke of Bergundy, Philippe le Bon, was said to have left more than half a million ounces of silver vessels of one sort or another. Of all this and very much more very little remains; what still exists now belongs almost wholly to great museums – such pieces as the Royal Gold Cup, Paris, 1380, in the British Museum, enamelled with the story of St Agnes. If, at the rarest intervals, a piece of domestic silver earlier than about 1500 should come on to the market it inevitably finds a permanent home in a national collection as did the Paris nef of 1482-3 which provides the frontispiece to this book.

In any case French silver is rare, for war and revolution have taken toll throughout the centuries and the financial difficulties of the Crown towards the end of the reign of Louis XIV brought a great deal to the melting pot. The result has been that much of the finest French silver is to be seen outside France rather than in its country of origin, and the influence of French design upon the silversmiths of other countries, notably England, especially during the last years of the seventeenth and the first half of the eighteenth century has been marked if not always recognised. It has sometimes been argued that the change in style which is so evident in the domestic silver of England from about the 1690s onwards is due wholly to the French Huguenot silversmiths who left their native land after the Revocation of the Edict of Nantes in 1685. As a result French Protestants were no longer able to follow their religion, and many hundreds of good craftsmen emigrated, to the lasting advantage of Germany, Holland and England. It seems more likely that the change of fashion would have come about even if Louis XIV, under the influence of the bigoted Madame de Maintenon, had not agreed to the persecution of his Calvinist subjects, for the cultural influence of the French capital and the prestige of the Sun King were prodigious. None of France's neighbours could fail to be impressed, not merely by the power of France and by the splendour with which the monarch surrounded himself, but also by the high standard of all the applied arts. It was inevitable that the style initiated by such men as Paul Ducereau (c. 1630-1713), Jean Berain (1637-1711) and Jean Lepautre (1618-82) should spread beyond the borders of the kingdom. As far as silver-smiths were concerned, the ideas of these three industrious leaders of design were translated into forms suitable for silver by M.-P. Mouton of Lyons in *Livre de Desseins pour toute sorte d'Ouvrages d'Orfèvrerie* and by Masson in *Nouveaux Desseins d'Ouvrage pour Graver sur l'Orfèvrerie*. Such patterns would have inevitably crossed the channel even without the agency of disgruntled exiles if for no other reason than that the patrons of the London silversmiths would demand the latest from Paris. It is odd to discover that while the fashion after the Restoration of Charles II in 1660 was largely based upon Dutch examples – this applied more to furniture than to silver – the arrival of a Dutch king in 1698 shifted the emphasis to France. This was no doubt partly due to the influence of Daniel Marot, himself a Huguenot refugee to Holland, who spent some time in England in the service of King William, and it was now that the high standard of craftsmanship of the French emigrés began to make itself felt. The embossed flowers for instance, so engaging a feature of the silver of the reigns of Charles II and James II began to go out. Ornament began to be applied, not hammered out, though gadrooning and fluting were still produced by the old method, and it seems certain that the immigrants, thanks to their training in France, were at this stage more skilful than their English competitors, who took fright immediately and did what they could to make life difficult for them. John Evelyn, in his diary entry for 3 November 1685, has this to say about our attitude: 'The French persecution of the Protestants raging with the utmost barbarity, exceeded even what the very heathens used,' a statement which does more credit to the diarist's heart than to his head; he exaggerates both numbers and the extent of the disaster, though that was bad enough (e.g. 'France was almost dispeopled ... manufactures ceased') but he does say this, that the exiles in England 'found least encouragement, by a fatality of the times we were fallen into and the uncharitable indifference of such as should have embraced them; and I pray it not be laid to our charge'. While no doubt there was any amount of amiable goodwill available, practical help was another thing entirely. The Goldsmiths' Company was quick to register alarm when the first trickle of immigrants came to London even before the Revocation. The newcomers could not sell their wares without having them assayed at Goldsmiths Hall, and the Company relied upon their fourteenth-century Charter by which only Freemen of the Company were entitled to this privilege. Consequently a newcomer had either to work for a London Master or induce the Company to mark his silver. Pierre Harache was the first French silversmith to be admitted to the Company. That was in 1682. But later the Court and the Wardens sometimes adopted a less rigid attitude, allowing men to have their work assayed while continuing to refuse admission to the Freedom. The wrangle continued for some years with varying results until it was finally decided in 1725 that the Company, in spite of their Charter, could not refuse to mark plate brought by those who were not members. The real point was that the immigrants had evidently improved the standard of workmanship but, because of their difficult situation, had not demanded higher prices. Standards were bound to become higher because French fashions demanded cast instead of embossed work, and so the English silversmiths necessarily accepted the higher standards lest they lose their market. But for all the heartburning during these years it is still likely that even without Louis XIV's persecution the London trade would have adopted the new designs. Soon, of course, the newcomers were absorbed into the population and we hear no more of anti-Huguenot prejudices.

Makers' Marks, Date Letters, Charge and Discharge Marks, etc.

Newcomers to the pleasure inseparable from the study of silver are liable to find a detailed explanation of the marks used by French silversmiths over three or four centuries exasperating and bewildering, requiring far more attention than has to be given to English silver. It will therefore be no insult to the author if the majority of those who open this book shudder slightly at what follows and, without pursuing the problem further, consult the few experts who have actually handled French silver all their lives and have thus acquired the necessary expertise to pronounce judgment upon the endless anomalies, exceptions, oddities and fantasies of the system. This is not a reference book *à la* Nocq, or Carré or Helft, but merely an attempt by means of words of one syllable as far as possible and by reproductions of actual marks to lay down basic principles. For the latter one is indebted to Diderot's great eighteenth century *Encyclopédie*, for the former – (the marks themselves) – as reproduced in the standard works from Nocq down to our own day. Wherever possible the marks on the actual objects illustrated have been photographed and are seen beside the pieces to which they belong. The amateur will sometimes no doubt find it difficult to decipher them; he may take comfort from the fact that, though all those illustrated can be read by experts with ease, there are hundreds of others which, thanks to the ravages of time, carelessness on the part of the maker, changes in the system, or occasionally deliberate fraud still provide intriguing problems.

This goes back to an ordinance of 1275, confirmed in 1355, but evidently often disregarded. From the sixteenth century onwards, it is generally composed of letters from the maker's name – for instance FCB for François Corbie – and surmounted by a crowned fleur-de-lis. More than 7,500 silversmiths in Paris and the provincial centres are recorded. Of these the marks of only twenty-four are reproduced here as examples:

Auguste, Henry. Master 1785, died 1816

Auguste, Robert-Joseph. Master 1757, mentioned 1795

Ballin, Claude II. Master 1688, died 1754

Balzac, Edmé Pierre. Master 1739

Besnier, Nicolas. Master 1714, died 1754

Biennais, Martin-Guillaume. 1764–1843   *Biennais*

Cousinet, Henry-Nicolas. Master 1725, died 1768

Duguay, Jacques. Master 1726, died 1749

Durand, Antoine-Sébastien. Master 1740, mentioned 1785

Fauche, Jean. Master 1733, died about 1762

Germain, Thomas. Master 1720, died 1748

Germain, François-Thomas. Master 1748, died 1791

Germain, Pierre, (le Romain). Master 1744, died 1783

Gouel, Gilles-Claude. Master 1727, died 1769

Huguet, Jean-Vincent. Master 1745, mentioned 1786

Igonet, Sébastien. Master 1725, mentioned 1766

Lenhendrick, Louis-Joseph. Master 1747, died 1783

Loir, Alexis III. Master 1733, died 1775

Odiot, Jean-Baptiste-Claude. 1763–1850

Outrebon, Jean-Louis. Master 1772, mentioned 1789

Outrebon, Nicolas II. Master 1735, died 1779

Regnard, Louis. Master 1733, died 1779

Roëttiers, Jacques. Master 1733, retired 1772

Roëttiers, Jacques-Nicolas. Master 1765, retired about 1777

After 22 November 1506 the Wardens of the Silversmiths Guild (*La Maison Commune*) were allotted by law the duty of stamping works of precious metal after assay. The system of date letters began in 1472 – crowned letters which change each year at the election of the Wardens. Until 1661 these elections were held in December, afterwards in July or August. The letter J was ignored, and so was U until 1783. In that year the U was used for the first time, but in 1784 until 1789 a crowned P with the last two figures of the year was adopted. The letters of the alphabet came round in 23, 24, or 25 years.

As sixteenth and seventeenth century silver is so rarely seen, the Warden's marks and date letters are given here for the eighteenth century only.

1697 – 1704 C,D,E,F,G,H,I,K	1727 – 1732 L,M,N,O,P,Q	1762 – 1768 Y,Z,A,B,C,D,E
1704 – 1711 K,L,M,N,O,P,Q,R	1732 – 1738 Q,R,S,T,V,X,Y	1768 – 1775 E,F,G,H,I,K,L,M
1711 – 1713 S,T,V	1738 – 1744 Y,Z,A,B,C,D	1775 – 1781 M,N,O,P,Q,R
1714 – 1717 X,Y,Z	1744 – 1750 D,E,F,G,H,I,K	1781 – 1783 R,S,T
1717 – 1722 A,B,C,D,E	1750 – 1756 K,L,M,N,O,P,Q	1783 – 1789 T,U, then P84 to P88
1722 – 1727 E,F,G,H,I,K,L	1756 – 1762 Q,R,S,T,V,X,Y	1789

The charge mark was stamped by the Wardens when the silversmith took his work to be assayed. The discharge mark was stamped by the tax-farmer when the tax was paid. (The letter A, in the examples shown in Appendix 2, was the privilege of Paris; it is not a date letter.) Other districts used the following letters:

Paris

Dates	Charge	Discharge
1697 – 1704		
1704 – 1711		
1711 – 1713		
1714 – 1717		
1717 – 1722		
1722 – 1727		

Paris

Dates	Charge		Discharge		
1727 – 1732					
1732 – 1738					
1738 – 1744					
1744 – 1750					
1750 – 1756					
1756 – 1762					
1762 – 1768					
1768 – 1775					
1775 – 1781					

Paris

Dates	Charge	Discharge
1781 – 1783		
1783 – 1789		1783 – 1786 1786 – 1789
1789		

Appendix 4   *List of Letters and Districts*

A	Paris	P	Dijon
B	Rouen	Q	Perpignan
C	Caen	R	Orléans
D	Lyon	S	Reims
E	Tours	T	Nantes
F	Angers	V	Troyes
G	Poitiers	X	Amiens
H	La Rochelle	Y	Bourges
I	Limoges	Z	Grenoble
K	Bordeaux	&	Aix
L	Bayonne	AA	Metz
M	Toulouse	CC	Besançon
N	Montpellier	W	Lille
O	Riom	9	Rennes

In the provinces the arms of the town or its initials were often used in the Warden's marks and often combined with the initials of the makers.

In 1791 the Silversmiths Corporation (the Paris equivalent of the London Worshipful Company in Foster Lane with its ancient duties of assay) was abolished in the name of liberty and with it the tax farmer who had long outlived any useful function he might once have had. It was soon found that it was essential to re-establish some form of control and this was done in 1797. Tax was henceforth collected by the State, and the State guaranteed the standard (*titre*). Pieces made just before or during the Revolution but put on the market only after several years will often bear both the normal marks of the old method and the marks set out in the following diagrams.

DATES	GOLD	SILVER
1793 – 1794	No mark	
1795 – 1797	 2nd standard  3rd standard	  1st standard 2nd standard
1797	Probably no marks	 1st standard
1798 until 19 June	 1st, 2nd and 3rd standard  Small objects	 1st, 2nd and 3rd standard  Small objects

85

DATES	GOLD		SILVER	
	PARIS	DEPARTMENT	PARIS	DEPARTMENT
Standard				
-1798 – 1809-				
Guaranty				
Standard				
-1809 – 1819-				
Guaranty				

DATES	GOLD		SILVER	
	PARIS	DEPARTMENT	PARIS	DEPARTMENT
Standard				
1819 – 1838				
Guaranty				
Standard Since 1879				
From 1838				
	Since 1838 Since 1879		Since 1838	
Guaranty	ET Export	Import		

List of Paris Silversmiths

ADNET, Henry. Master 1712, d. 1745.
ALLAIN, Henry. Master 1745, d. between 1755–1766.
ALLEN, Jacques-Louis. Master 1758, d. 1783.
ANDRÉ, David. Master 1703, d. before 1743.
ANDRIEUX, Jean-Baptiste. 1st half 19th century.
ANTHIAUME, Jacques. Master 1758, d. 1784.
ANTHIAUME, Louis-Julien. Master 1779, mentioned 1793.
ANTOINE, Léopold. Master 1706.
AUBRY, Claude-Auguste. Master 1758, mentioned 1791.
AUGUSTE, Henry. Master 1785, d. 1816.
AUGUSTE, Robert-Joseph. Master 1757, mentioned 1795.
BAILLY, Antoine. Master 1748, d. 1765.
BALLIN, Claude 11. Master 1688, d. 1754.
BALLIN, Jacques. Master 1750, d. 1764.
BALZAC, Edmé-Pierre. Master 1739, no record after 1780.
BALZAC, Jean-François. Master 1749, d. about 1766.
BARRY, Thomas-Michel. Mark 1798.
BASTIER, Jean. Master 1764, d. 1711.
BASTIN, Jean-Nicolas. Master 1774, d. 1785.
BATAILLE, Charles-Nicolas. Master 1738, d. 1759.
BELLANGER, Joseph. Master 1726.
BELLANGER, Louis. Master 1718, d. 1755.
BERGER, Louis-Jacques. mentioned 1806.
BERTHE, Julien. Master 1722, mentioned 1757.
BERTHE, Martin. Master 1712.
BERTHET, Jean-Baptiste-François. 1st half 19th century.
BERTIN, Antoine. Master 1700.
BERTIN, Jean-Baptiste. Master 1740, d. 1771.
BERTIN, Nicolas. Master 1644, mentioned 1699.
BERTIN, Nicolas. Master 1702.
BERTRAND, F.-J. 1st half 19th century.
BESNIER, Jacques. Master 1720, d. 1761.
BESNIER, Nicolas. Master 1714, d. 1754.

BEYDEL, Jacques-Laurent. Mark 1797.

BIENNAIS, Martin-Guillaume. born 1764, d. 1843.

BIBRON, Jean-Pierre. Mark 1798.

BOISSIÉRE, Jean-Claude. Master 1720, mentioned 1752.

BOISSIÉRE, Louis-Constant de la. Master 1759.

BOMPART, Jacques-Gabriel-André. Mark 1798.

BONHOMME, Jacques-Antoine. Master 1777.

BOUILLEROT, Charles-Antoine. Master 1769.

BOUILLEROT, Jean-Louis. Master 1761.

BOUILLEROT, Joseph. Master 1759.

BOULANGER, Jean-Nicolas. Master 1783.

BOULANGER, Simon. Master 1691, d. 1715.

BOULLIER, Antoine. Master 1775, mentioned 1806.

BOURGEOIS, Antoine. Master 1708.

BOURGEOIS, Charles-Louis. Mark 1798.

BOURGOIN, Denis. Master 1777.

BOURGUET, Jean-Antoine. Master 1758, mentioned 1785.

BOURGUET, Simon. Master 1740, d. before 1773.

BOUTHEROUE-DESMARAIS, César-Charles. Master 1731, d. 1758.

BOUTHEROUE-DESMARAIS, César-Louis. Master 1764.

BOUTHEROUE-DESMARAIS, Noël-César. Master 1764.

BRÉANT, Vincent. Master 1754.

BRICART, Nicolas-Pierre. Mentioned 1806.

BRISSON, Charles. Master 1761.

CAHIER, Jean-Charles. Born 1772, retired 1849.

CARRON, François-Alexis. Master 1777.

CARRON, Jean-François-Nicolas. Master 1755, mentioned 1806.

CASTAIN, Charles-Ignace. Master 1726, mentioned 1758.

CHABROL, Jean. Master 1709, d. about 1765.

CHARLIER, Brice. Master 1704, mentioned 1766.

CHARPENAT, Jean-Pierre. Master 1782, d. before 1806.

CHARTIÉ, Charles-Michel. Mentioned 1809.

CHARVET, Claude. Master 1728, d. 1751.

CHARVET, Claude-Antoine. Master 1757, d. 1782.

CHARVET, Joseph. Master 1751, d. before 1770.

CHATRIA, Rémy. Master 1724, d. 1744.

CHAYÉ, Antoine. Master 1747, d. 1754.

CHAYÉ, Germain. Master 1755, d. after 1787.

CHAZERAY, François. Master 1760, mentioned 1793.

CHÉRET, Jean-Baptiste-François. Master 1759, mentioned 1791.

CHÉRET, Pierre-Henry. Master 1741, d. 1787.

CHÉRET, Simon. Master 1716.

CHÉZELLE, Jean-Pierre. Master 1745, d. 1771.

H

CLÉRIN, Lazare-Antoine. Master 1741, d. 1782.
COLLIER, Nicolas. Master 1766, mentioned 1793.
COLOMBIER, Augustin-Barthélemy. Master 1781, mentioned 1793.
COLOMBIER, Denis. Master 1776, mentioned 1806.
COPPIN, Claude. Master 1725, d. 1753.
COPPIN, François. Master 1682, mentioned 1725.
CORBIE, François. Master 1777, mentioned 1793.
CORDIER, Louis. Master 1692, retired 1748.
CORNU, Nicolas. Master 1770, mentioned 1789.
COURTOIS, Etienne-Auguste. 1st half 19th century.
COUSINET, Ambroise-Nicolas. Master 1745, d. 1788.
COUSINET, Henry-Nicolas. Master 1725, d. 1768.
CROCHET, Nicolas. Master 1720, d. between 1748–1751.
CROZE, Charles-François. Master 1712, retired 1754.
CROZE, Georges-Antoine. Master 1777, mentioned 1790.
DANDRIEUX, Nicolas. Master 1716, mentioned 1764.
DANY, Alexis. Master 1758, mentioned 1793.
DANY, Roch-Louis. Master 1779, mentioned 1806.
DAPCHER, Jean-François. Master 1751, d. about 1776.
DARDET, Bonaventure. Master 1739, mentioned 1793.
DARDET, Claude-Gabriel. Master 1715.
DARGENT, Claude. Master 1722, mentioned 1771.
DAUMY, Jacques. Master 1783, mentioned 1806.
DEBRIE, Henri-Nicolas. Master 1758, mentioned 1791.
DEBRIE, Jacques. Master 1777, d. 1782.
DEBRIE, Jean. Master 1725, d. 1758.
DEFER, Jean-François. Master 1766, mentioned 1789.
DEHARCHIES, Claude. Master 1758, mentioned 1791.
DEHARCHIES, Jean. Master 1720, d. between 1765–1766.
DELANOIS, Claude-Nicolas. Master 1766, mentioned 1793.
DELANOIS, Jean-François. Master 1785, mentioned 1793.
DELAPIERRE, François. Master 1758, mentioned 1791.
DELAPIERRE, Michel 11. Master 1737, mentioned 1785.
DELARBRE, Louis-Philippe. Master 1719, retired 1752.
DELAROCHE, Jean-Jacques. Master 1723, d. 1778.
DELAUNAY, Nicolas. Master 1672, d. 1727.
DELAUNAY, Pierre-Antoine. Master 1770, mentioned 1789.
DELAVIGNE, Jacques. Master 1714.
DELISLE, Pierre. Master 1752, d. 1775.
DEMAY, Jacques-Joseph. Master 1769.
DEMAY, Louis-Philippe. Master 1758, d. 1772.
DEPRIS, Alexandre. Master 1714, d. 1731.
DESMAZURES, Michel-François. Master 1729.

DESMAZURES, Thomas. Master 1713, mentioned 1766.
DESSEMET, Claude. Master 1731, retired about 1766.
DEVAUX, Louis-Pierre. Master 1752, retired 1756.
DODARD, Jacques-François. Master 1779, mentioned 1793.
DOLIN, Nicolas. Master 1647, d. 1695.
DONZE, Charles. Master 1756, d. 1777.
DOUTÉ, Henri-Jean. Master 1767, in the provinces 1781.
DUBOIS, Antoine-Henry. Mark 1797.
DUBOIS, Jacques. Master 1779, mentioned 1793.
DUCHESNE, Jean-Charles. Master 1767, mentioned 1793.
DUCHESNE, Charles. Master 1738, d. 1753.
DUGUAY, Jacques. Master 1726, d. 1749.
DUGUAY, Joseph-Pierre-Jacques. Master 1756, mentioned 1793.
DUQUESNOY, Noël. Master 1694.
DURAND, Antoine-Sébastien. Master 1740, mentioned 1785.
DURAND, Louis. Master 1724, d. 1751.
DURIER, Nicolas. Master 1758, d. 1788.
DURU, Jean-Christophe. Master 1721, d. 1752.
DUTRY, Antoine. Master 1767, mentioned 1788.
DUVIVIER, Claude. Master 1720, mentioned 1766.
ECOSSE, Jean. Master 1705, d. about 1743.
EGÉE, Guillaume. Master 1716, d. 1759.
FAMECHON, Jacques. Master 1770, mentioned 1785.
FAMECHON, Pierre-Antoine. Master 1785, mentioned 1792.
FAUCHE, Jean. Master 1733, d. about 1762.
FAUCONNIER, Nicolas. Master 1785.
FAVIER, Claude-Eustache. Master 1732, mentioned 1748.
FAVIER, Louis. Master 1688, mentioned 1712.
FAVIER, Louis-Pierre. Master 1756, mentioned 1793.
FAVRE, Jacques. Master 1774, mentioned 1793.
FERRIER, René-Pierre. Master 1775, mentioned 1793.
FILASSIER, Antoine. Master 1704, mentioned 1759.
FILLASSIER, Jacques. Master 1718.
FILASSIER, Michel. Master 1694, d. before 1745.
FLORAT, Marc-Laurent. Master 1699.
FRANCKSON, Denys. Master 1765, mentioned 1791.
FRANCKSON, Denis-François. 1st half 19th century.
GABRIEL, Louis-Emmanuel. Master 1773, mentioned 1783.
GAILLARD, Jean. Master 1695, suspended 1754.
GARAND, Jean-François. Master 1748, d. 1778.
GARBE, Philippe-Emmanuel. Master 1748, mentioned 1793.
GASTELLIER, Jean-Médard. Master 1769, d. 1783.
GAUCHER, Claude-François. Master 1728, d. 1756.

GAVET, François-Charles. Mentioned 1806.

GENU, Jean-François. Master 1754, d. 1781.

GENU, Marie-Joseph-Gabriel. Master 1788, mentioned 1806.

GEORGES, Marie-Gabriel. Master 1745, d. 1775.

GEORGEON, Bernard. Master 1779.

GERBU, Gabriel. Master 1782, mentioned 1806.

GERFAUX, Michel-François. Master 1769, mentioned 1793.

GERMAIN, François-Thomas. Master 1748, d. 1791.

GERMAIN, Pierre. Master 1744, d. 1783.

GERMAIN, Thomas. Master 1720, d. 1748.

GILLET, Jean-Baptiste. Master 1734, d. 1786.

GIRARD, Charles. Master 1722, mentioned 1759.

GIROUX, Abel-Etienne. Mentioned 1806.

GODIN, Edmé-François. Master 1747, d. 1760.

GOGLY, Jean-François. Master 1762, mentioned 1793.

GOGLY, Pierre-François. Master 1768, mentioned 1793.

GONTHIER, Nicolas. Master 1768, mentioned 1793.

GORDIÉRE, Jean-Charles. Master 1747.

GOVAERS, Daniel. Master 1717, bankrupt 1736, d. before 1754.

GOVEL, Gilles. Master 1694, mentioned 1754.

GOVEL, Gilles-Claude. Master 1727, d. 1769.

GOVEL, Jean. Master 1722, mentioned 1739.

GRANGERET, Pierre-François. 1st half 19th century.

GRÉBEUDE, Jacques-François. Master 1711.

GRESSET, Louis-Joseph. Master 1781, mentioned 1793.

GRIMPRELLE, Charles. Master 1786, mentioned 1793.

GUÉRIN, Eloy. Master 1727.

GUIGNARD, André-Alexandre. Master 1782, mentioned 1793.

GUIART, Etienne. Master 1712, d. 1751.

HAMON, Martin. Master 1720.

HANNIER, Guillaume. Master 1723, d. about 1755.

HANNIER, Guillaume-Claude. Master 1773, mentioned 1787.

HANNIER, Jean. Master before 1679.

HANNIER, Jean. Master 1756, d. about 1781.

HANNIER, Jean-Nicolas. Master 1727, mentioned 1766.

HANNIER, Pierre. Master 1716.

HAUDRY, Antoine. Master 1718, d. before 1748.

HAUDRY, Charles-César. Master 1732, d. before 1762.

HÉRICOURT, Claude. Master 1763, mentioned 1785.

HIENCE, Antoine. Mentioned 1806.

HOART, Louis. Master 1720, d. 1745.

HOART, Pierre-Denis. Master 1771, mentioned 1793.

HOUSSEAU, François. Master 1705.

HOUSSEAU, Jean-Baptiste. Master 1703.

HOUTMAN, Antoine-Nicolas. Mentioned 1806.

HUGUET, Jean-Simon. Master 1752, mentioned 1791.

HUGUET, Jean-Vincent. Master 1745, mentioned 1786.

HUGUET, Philippe-Jean-Baptiste. Mentioned 1806.

HYON, Pierre-Louis. 1st half 19th century.

IGONET, Sébastien. Master 1725, mentioned 1766.

IMBERTY, Jacques-Antoine-Félix. Master 1777, mentioned 1786.

JACOB, François. Master 1636, d. 1695.

JACOB, Guillaume. Master 1666, mentioned 1715.

JACOB, Guillaume-Alexis. Master 1745, mentioned 1781.

JACQUART, Marc. Mentioned 1806.

JANETY, Marc-Etienne. Master 1777, mentioned 1793.

JARRIN, Pierre. Master 1712.

JARRY, Richard. Master 1708, d. 1759.

JOITTEAU, Pierre-Lucien. Master 1773, mentioned 1793.

JOSSET, Julien. Master 1767.

JOUBERT, Aymé. Master 1703, d. before 1747.

JOUBERT, Daniel-Jean. Master 1745, no record after about 1763.

JOUBERT, François. Master 1749, mentioned 1793.

JOUBERT, Pierre-Aymé. Master 1735, left Paris in 1763.

JOUVET, Antoine. Master 1783, mentioned 1793.

JULLIOT, Jean-Edmé. Master 1772, mentioned 1791.

LACOMPART, Christophe-François. Master 1717, d. 1751.

LACROIX, Claude. Master 1780, mentioned 1793.

LAGET, Noël-Charles. Master 1728, no record after 1759.

LAGNEAU, Thomas-Léonor. Master 1722, no record after 1748.

LAMICHE, François. Master 1717, no record after 1753.

LAMICHE, Nicolas. Master 1702.

LANDELLE, Pierre. Master 1705, d. 1753.

LANGE, Jean. Master 1677, shut down before 1702.

LANGE, Jean-Baptiste. Master 1706, d. 1750.

LANGLOIS, Jean-Etienne. Master 1770, mentioned 1793.

LANGLOIS, Marcoult. Master 1715, shut down 1766.

LANGLOIS, Nicolas-Martin. Master 1757, mentioned 1789.

LANGLOIS, Noël-Charles. Master 1708, d. 1748.

LANGLOIS, Philippe-Jacques. Master 1708, d. before 1748.

LANIER, Nicolas. Master 1714, shut down before 1748.

LASSUS, Michel de. Master 1720, d. 1772.

LAURENT, Claude. Master 1724, d. 1746.

LAUTRAN, Charles-François. Master 1762, d. 1777.

LEBARBIER, Joseph. Master 1720.

LEBLOND, Edmé-Paul. Master 1699, mentioned 1715.

LEBLOND, Edouard. Master 1700, mentioned 1727.
LEBLOND, Sébastien. Master 1674, mentioned 1715.
LEBRET, Etienne. Master 1669, mentioned 1689.
LEBRUN, Antoine. Master 1702, d. 1758.
LEBRUN, Jean-Baptiste. Master 1771, mentioned 1790.
LEBRUN, Marc-Augustin. 1st half 19th century.
LECLERC, Hugues. Master 1717, mentioned 1742.
LECLERC, Pierre. Master 1748, shuts down 1765.
LÉCUYER, Louis-Guillaume. Master 1746, d. 1758.
LEDOUX, Guillaume. Master 1705, d. 1751.
LEGAST, Charles-François. Master 1769, mentioned 1793.
LEGRAND, Jean-Louis. Master 1781, mentioned 1793.
LEGROS, Louis. Master 1723, shuts down 1736.
LEGROS, Louis-Edouard. Master 1746, shuts down 1753.
LEGUAY, Jacques-Louis-Auguste. Master 1779, mentioned 1806.
LEMAIRE, Charles-Etienne. Master 1759, mentioned 1781.
LEMIRE, Claude. Master 1725, shuts down 1751.
LEMOYNE, Marien. Master 1715, d. 1770.
LEMOYNE, René-Jean. Master 1775, mentioned 1793.
LENHENDRICK, Louis-Joseph. Master 1747, d. 1783.
LÉONARD, Noël. Master 1714, d. 1765.
LERICHE, Jean-Charles. Master 1745, d. 1754.
LEROY, Marc-Antoine. Master 1769, mentioned 1793.
LEROY, Nicolas. Master 1651, d. 1699.
LÉVESQUE, Louis-Antoine. Master 1753, mentioned 1791.
L'HONOREY, David. Master 1782, mentioned 1807.
LINZELER, Charles-Auguste. About 1820.
LOIR, Alexis III. Master 1733, d. 1775.
LOIR, Guillaume. Master 1716, shuts down towards 1767.
LOIR, Jean-Baptiste. Master 1689, d. 1716.
LOQUE, Jean-Ange. Master 1777, mentioned 1806.
LOQUE, Louis. 1st half 19th century.
LORILLON, Cincinnatus. 1st half 19th century.
LORILLON, Pierre-Benoît. 1st half 19th century.
LOYSEAU, Pierre. Master 1712, d. before 1759.
LUCAS, Antoine. Master 1770, mentioned 1803.
MAHON, Nicolas. Master 1719, d. 1733.
MAILLY, Louis. Master 1723, d. 1739.
MAINGENEAU, Jean-Louis. Master 1727, d. before 1748.
MALQUIS-LEQUIN, Jacques. Master 1735, mentioned 1790.
MANAUT, Louis. 1st half 19th century.
MARCAULT, Marcelin. Master 1732, d. 1771.
MARCAULT, Pierre-Nicolas. Master 1733, d. 1789.

MARCQ, Etienne-Jacques. Master 1732, d. 1781.

MARIE, Marin. Master 1656, d. before 1699.

MARTEAU, Jacques-Pierre. Master 1757, d. 1779.

MARTIN, Claude. Master 1637, d. 1682.

MARTIN, Jean-Baptiste. Master 1714.

MASSÉ, Pierre. Master 1639, mentioned 1690.

MASSÉ, Ange-Jacques. Master 1780, mentioned 1793.

MASSON, Nicolas-Richard. Mentioned 1806.

MAUVOISIN, Etienne. Master 1731.

MAUZIÉ, Jean. Master 1723, mentioned 1759.

MEISSONNIER, Juste-Aurèle. Master 1725, d. 1750.

MÉNIÈRE, Jean-Nicolas. Master 1770.

MÉNIÈRE, Nicolas. Master 1758, mentioned 1770.

MERCIER, Jean-Baptiste. Master 1696, d. 1745.

MERGER, Bertin. Master 1695, mentioned 1750.

MEUNAUST, Jean-Louis. Master 1760.

MEUNIEZ, Maurice. Master 1720, shuts down about 1745.

MEUSNIER, René. Master 1703, d. 1720.

MICALEF, Alexis. Master 1756.

MILLERAUD-BOUTY, Louis-Joseph. Master 1779.

MODENZ, Etienne. Master 1777, mentioned 1793.

MOILLET, Gabriel-Joseph. Master 1706, d. 1757.

MOILLET, Joseph. Master 1695, mentioned 1726.

MONGENOT, Edmé-Joseph. Master 1767, mentioned 1790.

MONGENOT, Jacques-Charles. Master 1775, mentioned 1790.

MOREAU, Etienne. Master 1753, mentioned 1790.

MOREL, Jean-Louis. Master 1748, mentioned 1791.

MOTHÉ, Robert. Master 1704.

MOTHET, Pierre-Médard. Master 1761, mentioned 1791.

MOULINEAU, Claude-Alexis. Master 1718.

MOUTON, Pierre. Master 1642, mentioned 1589.

MOYNAT, Jean. Master 1745, retired 1761.

MOZAC, Pierre-Etienne-Claude. Master 1777, mentioned 1793.

NAUDIN, François-Dominique. Mentioned 1806.

NEUSÉCOURT, Noël. Master 1783.

NEUVE, Pierre-Edouard. Master 1750, mentioned 1768.

NICOLLE, Louis. Master 1666, mentioned 1694.

NOLIN, Jean-Baptiste. Master 1740.

ODIOT, Jean-Baptiste-Claude. Master 1785, d. 1850.

ODIOT, Jean-Baptiste-Gaspard. Master 1720, d. 1767.

OUTREBON, Jean-Louis-Dieudonné. Master 1772, mentioned 1789.

OUTREBON, Nicolas 11. Master 1735, d. 1779.

PAGNON, Etienne. Master 1773, mentioned 1783.

PARAUD, Pierre. Mentioned 1806.
PARIS, Jean-Etienne. Master 1736, d. 1773.
PARISY, Séverin. Master 1771, mentioned 1793.
PATU, Denis. Master 1668, shuts down 1703.
PERNELLE, Henry. Master 1787, mentioned 1793.
PETIT, Charles. Master 1659.
PETIT, Jean. Master 1646, mentioned 1689.
PETIT, Jean-Baptiste. Master 1698.
PETIT, Jacques. Master 1765, mentioned 1793.
PETIT or BOULOGNE-PETIT, Julien. Master 1765, mentioned 1793.
PICARD, François. Master 1784.
PICARD, Jean. Master 1652, mentioned 1699.
PICART, Jean-Nicolas. Master 1682, d. 1747.
PIGEON, Jérome. Master 1705.
PIGEON, Nicolas. Master 1717, mentioned 1729.
PIGERON, Guillaume. Master 1762, d. before 1776.
PIQUE, Jean-Nicolas. Master 1780, mentioned 1793.
PLOT, Antoine. Master 1729, d. 1772.
POISSON, Jean-François-Charles. Master 1775.
POLLET, Etienne. Master 1747, shuts down 1757.
POLY, Adrien. Master 1677, mentioned 1718.
PONTANEAU, Jean-Simon. Master 1776, mentioned 1793.
PORCHER, Alexis. Master 1725, mentioned 1776.
PORCHER, Charles. Master 1761, d. 1776.
PORCHER, Louis-Claude. Master 1762, mentioned 1791.
POTTIER, Claude-Pierre. Master 1778, mentioned 1806.
PRÉVOST, Claude-Nicolas. Master 1770.
PRÉVOST, Nicolas. Master 1742, mentioned 1790.
PRÉVOST, Pierre. Master 1672, mentioned 1716.
RAVACHÉ, Etienne-Nicolas. Master 1781, mentioned 1793.
RAVECHÉ, Antoine-Martin. Master 1772.
RECONSEIL, Théodore-Simon. Master 1720, d. 1761.
REGNARD, Louis. Master 1733, d. 1779.
REGNARD, Pierre-Louis. Master 1759.
REGNIER, Pierre-Auguste-Simon. Master 1772, d. 1826.
RIDÉ, Claude-Jean. Master 1755, shuts down 1777.
RIGAL, François. Master 1713, d. 1751.
RIGAL, François. Master 1720, d. 1764.
RIGAL, François. Master 1769, d. 1788.
RIGAL, Nicolas. Master 1741, d. 1790.
RIGAL, Pierre-François. Master 1770, mentioned 1789.
RION, Sixte-Simon. 1st half 19th century.
ROBERDAY, François. Master before 1754.

ROËTTIERS, Jacques. Master 1733, retired 1772.

ROËTTIERS, Jacques-Nicolas. Master 1765, retired before 1777.

ROLLAND, Guillaume-François. Master 1777.

ROQUILLET-DESNOYERS, Jean-Charles. Master 1772, mentioned 1793.

ROSNEL, Denis de. Master 1692, mentioned 1715.

ROUGEMAILLE, Philippe. Master 1686, mentioned 1715.

ROUMIER, Jean-François. Master 1788, mentioned 1793.

ROUSSEAU, Philippe. Master 1776.

ROUSSY, Alexandre de. Master 1758, shuts down 1792.

ROUSSY, Louis de. Master 1763, mentioned 1789.

SALLOT, Pierre-Guillaume. Master 1750, mentioned 1793.

SAURIN, Jean-Baptiste. Master 1774, mentioned 1793.

SAVARY, Louis. Master 1781, mentioned 1793.

SERGENT, Hiérome. Master 1659, mentioned 1694.

SEVIN, Pierre. Master 1756, mentioned 1790.

SIFFAIT, Pierre. Master 1752, mentioned 1781.

SIMONIN, Nicolas. Master 1720, d. 1757.

SOMMÉ, Claude. Master 1771, mentioned 1792.

SOMMÉ, Pierre-Nicolas. Master 1760, retired 1806.

SOUCHET, Claude-Hyacinthe-Nicolas. Master 1777, mentioned 1791.

SOULAINE, Paul. Master 1720, d. 1759.

SPIRE, Charles. Master 1736, mentioned 1788.

SPRIMAN, Charles-Louis-Auguste. Master 1775.

TESSIER, Jean-Charles. Master 1772, mentioned 1793.

THÉRY, Antoine. Master 1782, mentioned 1791.

THÉVENOT, Louis-Gaspard. Master 1735, mentioned 1768.

THIBARON, Jean. Master 1717, d. 1760.

THIERRY, Claude-François. Master 1775, mentioned 1793.

THOMAS DES LONGCHAMPS, Jean-Jacques. Master 1782.

TOURAILLON, Nicolas. Master 1739, mentioned 1783.

TRIOULLIER, C. 1st half 19th century.

TROUVÉ, Jacques. Master 1680, mentioned 1715.

TURMINE, Auguste-Gaspard. Master 1778, d. 1786.

TURPIN, Antoine. Master 1680, mentioned 1700.

TURPIN, Robert. Master 1704, d. 1712.

VALLIÈRES, Nicolas-Clément. Master 1732, shuts down 1775.

VALLIÈRES, Pierre. Master 1776, mentioned 1806.

VALLOT, Jean-Baptiste. Master 1742, shuts down 1781.

VANCOMBERT, Joseph-Théodore. Master 1770, mentioned 1787.

VIAL, Nicolas. Master 1781.

VIARDOT, Pierre. Master 1712, d. 1756.

VIAUCOURT, Pierre-Antoine. Master 1753, mentioned 1793.

VIGNÉ, Louis. Master 1736, mentioned 1783.
VILAIN, Nicolas-Hilaire. Master 1727, shuts down 1740.
VILLAIN, Jean. Master 1670, expelled 1694.
VILLECLAIR, Antoine-Jean de. Master 1750, d. 1764.
VILLEMSENS, Jean-François. Master 1771, mentioned 1793.
VONARMS, Claude-François. Master 1781, mentioned 1793.
WATTIAUX, Pierre-Joseph. Master 1756, mentioned 1791.
WYRIOT, Jean-Jacques. Master 1716, d. 1738.

Bibliography

Designs

Berain, Jean. *Reproduction complète de l'oeuvre de Jean Berain, époque Louis* XIV, edited by Armond Guérmet. Paris, n.d.

Germaine, Pierre II. *Eléments d'orfèvrerie.* Paris, 1748.

Marot, Daniel. *Nouveau livre de l'orfèvrerie.* The Hague, 1703.

Masson. *Nouveaux dessins pour graver sur l'orfèvrerie.* Paris, early eighteenth century.

Meissonnier, Juste-Aurèle. *Oeuvre. Paris,* 1723-35. Blom, N.Y.

General

Bapst, Germain. *L'orfèvrerie française à la cour de Portugal au* XVIIIe *siècle.* Paris, 1892.

Bapst, Germain. *Etudes sur l'orfèvrerie française au* XVIIIe *siècle : les Germain.* 1887.

Brault, Solange et Bottineau, Yves. *L'orfèvrerie française du* XVIIIe *siècle.* Paris, 1959.

Carré, Louis. *Les poinçons de l'orfèvrerie française.* 1928.

Connaissance des Arts. *Les grands orfèvres.* Paris, 1965.

Grandjean, Serge. *L'orfèvrerie du* XIXe *siècle en Europe.*

Hayward, J. F. *Huguenot Silver in England.* Faber. London, 1959.

Helft, Jacques. *Le poinçon des provinces françaises.*

Musée du Louvre and Musée de Cluny. *Catalogue de l'orfèvrerie du* XVIIe *du* XVIIIe *et du* XIXe *siècle.* Paris, 1958.

Nocq, Henry. *Le poinçon de Paris,* 5 vols. Paris, 1926-31.

Oman, Charles. *Mediaeval Silver Nefs.* Victoria and Albert Museum. London, 1963.

Taylor, Gerald. *Continental Gold and Silver.* The Connoisseur and Michael Joseph, London, 1967.

Taylor, Gerald. *Art in Silver and Gold.* Dutton Vista Picture Book, London, 1964; Dutton Books, 1964.

Taylor, Gerald. *Silver.* Pelican Books, London, 1956. Rev. ed. Penguin N.Y., 1964.

Exhibition Catalogues

New York. Dennis, Faith. Three Centuries of French Domestic Silver (Catalogue of the Exhibition of 1938) 2 vols. Metropolitan Museum of Art, 1960.

Paris. Musée des Arts Décoratifs.
Orfèvrerie française ancienne, 1926.
Orfèvrerie civile française (after 1798), 1929.
Orfèvrerie civile de province, 1936.
Trésors d'orfèvrerie du Portugal (the former royal collection, Lisbon) 1954
Louis XIV ; fastes et décors, 1960.
Trésors des églises de France, 1965.

This book is intended for the layman and does not pretend to be an exhaustive study. It will be obvious that the author is greatly indebted to the books listed above. It is, he thinks, curious that, apart from the admirable volumes by Faith Dennis describing the New York exhibition of 1938, nothing specifically about French silver, apart from magazine articles, appears to have been published in English until now.

Index